Praise for *W*

When I was president of K-LOVE radio we realized the need to innovate if we wanted to be a part of the future. Nick and Ali created a framework where we could excel at what we were currently doing and see a pathway into the future that would help us achieve our mission to move people closer to Christ. They took an uncertain future and showed us a roadmap to where we needed to go to continue being effective.

ALAN MASON, board member and former CEO at K-Love/Air1

When I was orbiting Earth on the International Space Station, looking back down from 240 miles above, it was clear that the challenges facing our planet would not be solved by doing things the way we have always done them. This is why *What Comes Next?* is such a critical book. Not only do Nick and Ali help you understand how the world is changing, but they teach you what to do about it.

RON GARAN, astronaut; author of *The Orbital Perspective, Railroad to the Moon,* and *Floating in Darkness*

What Comes Next? is readable, inspiring, sometimes technical, and extremely missional for anyone who feels responsible to lead other followers of Jesus into a preferable future. The lessons of yesterday and the insights of today are not enough for leading tomorrow. When you take the journey with Nick and Ali, you will get a new tool in your leadership tool bag that will help you shape the future.

BRUCE WESLEY, Senior Pastor, Clear Creek Community Church

Many leaders rely on intuition and that gut instinct to make decisions and plan for the future. That's part of what got them into the position they currently hold. The problem, however, is that they all too often miss key factors in decision-making, which end up undermining the execution of their plan. Enter *What Comes Next?* The Futures Framework presented in this book provides a thoughtful, thorough guide to help you identify and execute an informed and flexible strategy based on principles and possibilities.

BRITT TUCKER, pastor, Antioch Community Church, Central Houston

Global society has been shattered by an invisible virus. Bewildered pastors are shaking their heads in confusion and fright. Many believe God has decided to bring to a screeching halt "Churchianity." It sadly skewed from the biblical road of organic body life into the side ditch of impersonal organization. Nick and Ali have created a handbook for those who are ready to sew new garments to clothe Christ's bride. Just in time!

RALPH NEIGHBOUR, author of many books on cell churches; consultant; president, TOUCH Training Center

It is rare to find people who are as genuine, true to their beliefs, and willing to stand by them as Ali and Nick. Together, they have written such a simple but powerful book that describes how all of us can be true to our faith and yet achieve personal and professional success. I highly recommend you read this book before your next meeting, group project, or deadline. It will change your life. It did mine.

CHRIS VEIN, former Deputy United States Chief Technology Officer for Government Innovation, The White House

When I asked Nick and Ali to help pull together a team to create a twenty-year strategy, I never imagined the disruptive future that they would envision. Many times, strategies for the future are just straight lines from where an organization has been in the past. Their strategy built upon the past but was not constrained by the past. It envisioned the possibilities. They have pulled together a succinct and powerful framework to help organizations and individuals envision the possible futures.

STEVEN GONZALEZ, retired Deputy, NASA Advanced Planning Office

Did you know it is actually easier to invent the future than to predict the future? Like no other generation before us, we have the opportunity to create transformational change. Drawing from their experience in government, disaster relief, refugee care, tech startups, innovation hacks, and advancement of the kingdom, Nick and Ali provide the motivation and framework to actually craft the future we want to live in. This book will inform, inspire, and equip you to make a difference.

ERIC SWANSON, Leadership Network; coauthor of *The Externally Focused Church* and *To Transform a City*

Trying to lead an organization, church, or ministry of any size in this increasingly VUCA (volatile, uncertain, complex, and ambiguous) environment is challenging on many levels. Nick and Ali do us all a favor by laying out a road map in the Futures Framework to help us chart a way forward. Their message and tools are timely, insightful, and indispensable for those charged with leading others through these uncharted waters. If you're a leader, pick up this book and get busy designing your preferred future!

MICK MURRAY, author of *The Father's Heart: Knowing the God of the Bible as Father*

Love this book. I've had the privilege of working closely with Nick and Ali to build projects and scale networks. *What Comes Next?* brings their enthusiasm, biblical wisdom, and practical advice to anyone who yearns to see life differently and make a difference.

KEN COCHRUM, Vice President of Global Digital Strategies, Cru

What Comes Next? is timely and timeless. The Futures Framework is a practical method of discovering how to navigate this unpredictable world. Ali and Nick have tapped into their incredible wealth of knowledge and experience in leading leaders globally in future thinking and innovation and put it into a simple process. If you are like me and need help rethinking the future, invest in yourself or your team, and purchase this book.

JAMES KELLY, founder and CEO, FaithTech

"What comes next?" is a question many leaders are asking during a year with unexpected disruption, uncertainty, and challenges no one could have anticipated. Ali and Nick's timely Futures Framework will both inspire you and guide you to dream big with God. These explorers point us to unprecedented possibilities for our churches, organizations, ministries, and businesses. They not only help us focus forward with courage and hope, but they give us the structure we need to create the roadmap that will take us there. This book is a must-read for kingdom leaders desiring to step into the future with clarity and impact!

SUSAN RYAN, president, Amoveo Consulting

In a time of global instability and transition, Nick and Ali turn with hope and expectation to what's coming next. With both depth and pragmatism, they equip Christian leaders with a framework to align themselves for what God is doing now and in the future.

BEAU EGERT, entrepreneur and community leader

WHAT COMES NEXT?

*Shaping the Future
in an Ever-Changing World*

A GUIDE FOR CHRISTIAN LEADERS

NICHOLAS SKYTLAND
ALICIA LLEWELLYN

MOODY PUBLISHERS

CHICAGO

Edited by Ashleigh Slater
Interior Design: Puckett Smartt
Cover Design: Erik M. Peterson
Cover illustration of arrows copyright © 2020 by cgdeaw / iStock (1226568477). All rights reserved.
Author photo for Nicholas Skytland: Glenna Harding
Author photo for Alicia Llewellyn: Stephanie Eddy

Library of Congress Cataloging-in-Publication Data

Names: Skytland, Nicholas, author. | Llewellyn, Alicia, author.
Title: What comes next? : shaping the future in an ever-changing world : a guide for Christian leaders / Nicholas Skytland and Alicia Llewellyn.
Description: Chicago : Moody Publishers, [2021] | Includes bibliographical references. | Summary: "In What Comes Next?, you'll develop the capacity to guide your organization by shaping the future so that it can thrive. Strategists and innovation experts Nick Skytland & Ali Llewellyn provide a framework for us to lead as futurists and grow our businesses and ministries"-- Provided by publisher.
Identifiers: LCCN 2020031944 (print) | LCCN 2020031945 (ebook) | ISBN 9780802419668 (paperback) | ISBN 9780802498588 (ebook)
Subjects: LCSH: Leadership--Religious aspects--Christianity. | Christian leadership. | Change--Religious aspects--Christianity.
Classification: LCC BV4597.53.L43 S525 2020 (print) | LCC BV4597.53.L43 (ebook) | DDC 253--dc23
LC record available at https://lccn.loc.gov/2020031944
LC ebook record available at https://lccn.loc.gov/2020031945

Originally delivered by fleets of horse-drawn wagons, the affordable paperbacks from D. L. Moody's publishing house resourced the church and served everyday people. Now, after more than 125 years of publishing and ministry, Moody Publishers' mission remains the same—even if our delivery systems have changed a bit. For more information on other books (and resources) created from a biblical perspective, go to www.moodypublishers.com or write to:

Moody Publishers
820 N. LaSalle Boulevard
Chicago, IL 60610

1 3 5 7 9 10 8 6 4 2

Printed in the United States of America

Dedication

To Asher, Kai, and Adah, may you never forget
to dare mighty things.

To Krista, thank you for joining us on this grand adventure.

Contents

Foreword

Welcome to an amazing field guide for your better future! Over the last two decades I've worked with Christian leaders, church teams, and ministry innovators to create clarity. Sometimes it's about the mission or ministry model. Sometimes it's about a brand-new strategy or long-range dream. But it's always about using your one and only life to make the ultimate contribution for which God put you on earth.

Nick and Ali's contribution to us through *What Comes Next?* is nothing short of highly accessible genius. They are mavens of possibility and tried-and-true futurists. Their aim is to help you do more of what you do best by giving you a breakthrough master tool—the Futures Framework—that will expand your imagination and focus your next steps in our ever-changing and chaotic times.

Are you ready to scale your dreams? You will love the Futures Framework. Are you hammering out a digitally integrated ministry strategy for the first time? Use the Futures Framework today! Do you want more vital connection with your team? Let the Futures Framework bring its social savvy to your endeavors to create deeper meaning for, with, and through the communities you serve.

Many books for Christian leaders are either too simplistic or too complicated. The simplistic ones may bring good ideas or inspiring stories but don't help you think and act differently. The complicated ones may show you how smart the author is, but the content only bogs you down in your busy world. Nick and Ali have done the work and walk us across the razor's edge. *What Comes Next?* is stunningly simple yet profound; it's super-readable yet comprehensive. We desperately need more books like this today. It will be your guide for a lifetime of innovation for the glory of God.

In many ways for me this book's value is not a surprise. Nick and Ali are fervent servants of Christ, stellar thinkers, proven leaders, and bona fide consultants. I live in the shadow of the Johnson Space Center in Houston's Clear Lake Area. Nick happens to be an elder at my home church. He is the genuine rocket scientist next door you also love having at your backyard BBQ! I can testify firsthand that Nick and Ali aren't just brilliant minds; they live brightly for Jesus.

As you jump into the four forces and eight intersections of the Futures Framework, get ready for two things:

First, I believe God was preparing this book in advance for the unprecedented disruption that COVID-19 would bring to spiritual leaders worldwide. I hope you marvel at our Creator's orchestration of Nick and Ali's life calling for such a time as this.

Second, if you are generous enough to get a copy in the hands of your team and courageous enough to have honest, generative dialogue, I have no doubt that *What Comes Next?* will change the trajectory of your company, church, or ministry.

You are about to be reminded that you were created for vision. So don't hesitate to engage what comes next.

WILL MANCINI
Founder of the Future Church Company, author of *Future Church* and *God Dreams*

Introduction

AN INVITATION TO JOIN US ON AN ADVENTURE

Never be afraid to trust an unknown future to a known God.[1]

—CORRIE TEN BOOM

D o you know what comes next?

After this season is over, after the next deadline is met, after that audacious goal you've set is accomplished, what does the future hold for you and your organization, church, or ministry?

Over the years, it's a question we've asked Christian leaders such as yourself as we've worked with them to build, test, and launch new and innovative ideas into the world. And, what we've noticed is that, for many leaders, thinking about the future sometimes leaves them feeling exhausted, discouraged, or fearful. Maybe you can relate, and that's why you've picked up this book.

You may feel overwhelmed because you don't have time to think about what comes next. It feels impractical. You have bills to pay, deadlines to keep, and an organization to run. And, even if you did have extra minutes in your day, you aren't sure where you'd start. You can barely keep up with the latest breaking news story, software up-date, or global trend that's threatening to disrupt everything you're working to do.

Thinking about the future can also be discouraging. Maybe your current reality isn't what your former self once envisioned, so it seems pointless to imagine alternatives. The years have taught you that your plans rarely unfold as you anticipated.

If that's you, you aren't alone. Most of us have sacrificed and pre-pared hard for the future we eagerly worked toward. We listened to our parents, followed the advice of our mentors, read all the latest leadership books, made a strategic plan, and brought the right people onto our teams. Yet when it comes to the impact we hoped to have, it rarely looks like what we expected when we get there. On the few occasions when it does, we often feel in retrospect like it was as much serendipity as it was intentionality.

Our planning for the future often depends on an approach we learned in childhood. We draw a straight line from today to next year and prepare for the future based on our recent experiences, best guesses, and current gut feelings. We attempt to predict what's next based on our familiar past behaviors instead of on future possibilities. The problem with this is that the potential of this approach is limited by what we currently know and have personally experienced. We don't make room for the unknown and unfamiliar.

As we grow wiser and realize that none of us has a crystal ball that will predict the future, it can make us feel even more lost or irrelevant in a world that is relentlessly changing in unexpected ways. If we're honest with ourselves, we might admit we're worried that our clear and defined straight line is being erased altogether. Or, maybe we've been following the wrong line all this time?

The fear of uncertainty strikes us all at some point, especially when things don't go as we thought they would or should. But there's a better way to respond in this uncertain world. Rather than feel overwhelmed, discouraged, or fearful, we can approach the future as explorers. Explorers, by definition, are people who journey through the unfamiliar to learn about it. It's the explorers who sailed uncharted waters, discovered new lands, circumnavigated the globe, set foot on the moon, and ventured deep into space. Exploration requires being brave, overcoming your fears, and permitting yourself to take the first step.

As a leader, how can you do this? Let us share some of our story with you.

EMBRACING UNCERTAINTY

When we started working together in 2008, the world felt just as unpredictable as it does today. Our industry was changing, jobs were disappearing, and technology was disrupting everything. We faced a decision on whether to keep our heads down and trust that the future would follow the straight-line trajectory we expected or to embrace the uncertainty and hold on for the ride.

We decided to embrace the uncertainty. The thing was, we didn't like where we saw the line going. At the time, the American space program was struggling to reach a younger generation. We had a vision for a better future and a different way to engage everyone in exploration, but it was hard for others to see it too. We decided to jump in anyway, aware that we might fail. We focused on the future we wanted to help create, instead of letting the future simply happen to us.

The results were astounding! We discovered how to revolutionize the relationship between space exploration and the general public, which we'll share more about in later chapters. Our work touched hundreds of thousands of people all over the planet. More importantly, we learned that when we invite others into this adventure with us, God can do more through us collectively than we could ever do alone.

What was unique about *this* time, *this* idea, and *this* team? What helped us unlock new possibilities? What gave us the courage to be misunderstood, and to walk by faith and not by sight? Most of all, how did we know this idea *was* the right idea?

This book is all about looking boldly into the future, figuring out what is possible, and defining the way forward. It's a guide to help Christian leaders like you respond well to uncertainty and shape the future in an ever-changing world.

As Scripture reminds us, "Do not be anxious about anything, but in everything by prayer and supplication with thanksgiving let your requests be made known to God. And the peace of God, which surpasses all understanding, will guard your hearts and your minds in Christ Jesus" (Phil. 4:6–7). But how do you know what to request? How do you decide what goals to set? How do you anticipate a different type of future, and then line up your heart and mind with those expectations?

PLANNING FOR WHAT COMES NEXT

The Bible encourages us to prepare thoughtfully for the future. Whether you're a corporate executive or entrepreneur, a pastor, or a ministry leader, Scripture isn't silent on the benefits of contemplating and readying yourself for what's next. As a leader, you're advised, "Know well the condition of your flocks, and give attention to your herds" (Prov. 27:23). Scripture also says, "Prepare your work outside; get everything ready for yourself in the field, and after that build your house" (Prov. 24:27) and that "the plans of the diligent lead surely to abundance, but everyone who is hasty comes only to poverty" (Prov. 21:5). Success often comes in the wake of planning. Without planning, we risk going bankrupt—financially, relationally, emotionally, and spiritually.

Your industry or backstory may be different than ours, but as you read, we think you'll see yourself in the stories and situations we share. Just like us and the leaders we'll tell you about in this book, you have work to do, people to lead, and a vision to carry.

The world is continually changing around you, and your past success isn't guaranteed in the future. You must be ready to act, and this book will help you do that. As we've worked to engage everyone in exploration, we've found that most people don't know where to begin.

Once they have a framework in hand to imagine what's possible and a community to collaborate with along the way, they've jumped in quickly. We hope you will do the same.

Fellow leader, you are an explorer, and this is your invitation to go on an adventure with us. We'll be there with you every step, equipping you with a new way to prepare for the future and giving you practical examples from our past experiences to encourage you. All you have to do is take the first step. We promise that you'll never want to look back.

This is *our* future. We're all invited. See you there.

— Nick and Ali

PART 1:

NEARSIGHTED

1

THE FUTURE BELONGS TO THE CURIOUS

We keep moving forward—opening up new doors and
doing new things—because we're curious. And curiosity
keeps leading us down new paths.[1]

—WALT DISNEY

It was a cold, foggy October morning in 2000 when NASA astronaut
William "Bill" Shepherd waved goodbye to his wife and boarded the
bus headed toward the rocket launch area located in the desert steppe
in southern Kazakhstan. There was an unspoken tension in the cold
air on this historic day.

Bill was joined by two steely-eyed Russian cosmonauts, Yuri Gid-
zenko and Sergei Krikalev, as they boarded the Soyuz spacecraft. Just
a few hours later, they were hurling through the atmosphere, chasing
down the International Space Station, orbiting Earth at 17,500 miles
per hour.

Ever since that day, humans have continuously lived in space. In
its first two decades, the International Space Station has hosted more

than 230 residents from countries around the world. These space explorers have braved hundreds of spacewalks and conducted thousands of research investigations that have led to unparalleled improvements in life on Earth and life in space.[2]

The pioneers that designed the International Space Station envisioned a future where humans would live permanently in space in an orbiting laboratory that could be built in phases. They then found others who shared their vision for a better future—a future where anything was possible—and were willing to collaborate to make it happen. Today, this miraculous laboratory, one of the most massive structures ever built, is an incredible testimony to what's possible when you envision the future with creativity, ingenuity, and a willingness to dream big.

The International Space Station has had a long and productive life, but NASA and other commercial space partners have started to plan for its retirement to make way for the next chapter in the storied history of human space exploration. What do *you* think humanity should explore next? Where's the next new frontier?

These are tough questions, aren't they? There are innumerable options beyond just returning to the moon or landing humans on Mars. NASA could design a new rocket to go far beyond previous frontiers to a completely new and uncharted destination. On the other hand, our nation could reinvest those funds to address other critical needs that are unrelated to exploration like hunger, poverty, or education. Some question the value of our space program in light of these real issues on Earth, while others fervently believe that these other needs demonstrate the criticality of continuing to explore the universe beyond the one small planet we call home.

As we write this book, NASA is working on another bold vision for the future of human spaceflight. Instead of a laboratory that orbits Earth, they're envisioning a new type of space station that acts more like a spaceship.[3] This unique spacecraft will not only orbit Earth but can also be repositioned in orbit around the moon to serve as a home base and outpost for expeditions to the lunar surface. For the first time in history, humans will build a permanent presence 250,000 miles away from Earth. Could you have envisioned that?

You may not be a rocket scientist tasked with building the next spacecraft to fly to the farthest edges of our solar system, but you are leading an organization, church, or ministry that has a vital mission. You need to think about the future so you can uncover your biases, anticipate changes, avoid surprises, produce more creative options, and identify new opportunities.

As we've already discussed, it's easy to trust in what you can see with your eyes and deduct from your personal experience, but there's far more to be seen when you shift your perspective and walk by faith. We want to help you be a futurist by equipping you with new and creative ways to respond to a changing world around you. This will prepare you to anticipate what will happen next and show you how to use your unique perspective to develop a new set of possibilities, positioning you for the preferred future you want to see. And all of this starts by thinking like a child.

CHILDLIKE CURIOSITY

Kids are often the best futurists. We asked Nick's two elementary-aged sons what they imagined about the future of human space exploration. Like many kids their age, they envision spaceships, not space stations. They foresee us traveling deeper into the galaxy in reconfigurable ve-hicles that don't just orbit one planet, but that fly around our solar system in pursuit of the next discovery. Neither of them sees any reason to gallivant around our solar system for too long; they would much rather head straight to the farthest edges of the galaxy.

The desire to explore the unknown is innate in almost all of us, especially as children. Kids believe anything is possible. Their youth affords them a perspective of the world that's truly unconstrained. They're innately curious creatures who are born explorers. Without the same inhibitions that adults have developed over the years, children experiment, dream, and view the world with wonder and imagination.

One of the reasons kids are natural explorers is because they're willing to ask the questions that drive exploration. Even the smallest children unapologetically seek to understand the cause and effect of things around them because they want to understand. Think back on the last time you talked to a child in your life; how many times did they ask why?

We most often see children's curiosity in action when they play. Play is their primary method of discovering themselves and their environment. It's where they feed their curiosity. They figure out how things work without being told and try new things just to see what happens. Kids happily construct cities under an imagined ocean using a box of building blocks, they dream about what it's like to be the president for a day, they sing duets with talking tigers, and they'd love nothing more than to wake up in a bathtub full of gelatin. Creative play gives them a way to make sense of the world around them. Elementary-aged Bill, Sergei, and Yuri—long before they were spacefarers—undoubtedly looked through their telescopes and imagined what might be in the faraway skies.

Unless taught to notice, when children play, they also tend to lack preconceptions and biases. Kids are unselfconscious and happy to try new things. They delight in what they see, touch, and taste, and can enjoy a pillow fort or cardboard-box-turned-airplane as much as the real thing.

As adults, many of us have reined in the freedom we once practiced as children. We've unconsciously trained ourselves to value speed, safety, efficiency, convenience, and consistency. We read business books like *In Search of Excellence* and *Built to Last* that lead with the logic that to be like the other successful companies, we need to emulate those companies. Empirical evidence and certainty are key values.

We rely on answers that require the least work to find. We think it's about finding the right solution, so we spend little time exploring, playing, and asking our own *why* questions. As a result, we often close ourselves off from hope and possibility. Our rationality shackles our ability to play in an attempt to eliminate ambiguity. Things are happening so rapidly around us that venturing to cast a vision about "what might be" seems an act of futility and folly. There are more questions than answers, and we want the answers now.

Advances in technology help fulfill our need for certainty. Voice-controlled assistants give us immediate answers to almost any question we have. *For how long do you bake cookies? Who discovered Antarctica? What's on the calendar for tomorrow? How many astronauts are in space?* But, while our lives may feel easier and more defined, we slowly lose our ability to search, wonder, and uncover understanding through discovery. We become reticent and unable to envision a future beyond the here and now.

But what if we learned to think and play like children again? Imagine what would be possible if you could see the world as kids do: without limitations, preconceptions, bias, fear, self-consciousness, or isolation. You can.

DO YOU REMEMBER THE FIRST TIME YOU PICKED UP A KALEIDOSCOPE?

Like children, grown-up explorers have a pioneering spirit and intrinsic curiosity that help them journey into the unknown. With boldness and inquisitiveness, they navigate new frontiers, even when the future is blurry or opaque. They aren't deterred when they can't see beyond the horizon . . . instead, they're often even more intrigued.

You too can be an explorer with the ability to dream and envision what's on the other side of the obstacles, challenges, and cultural realities you face. The future belongs to the curious, and by considering and changing your perspective, this can include you.

One of our favorite tools to help you deepen your field of vision is a kaleidoscope. Kaleidoscopes have been around since the 1800s.

You may remember the first time you peered through the faceted and prism-like lens of one as a child. Light bounced off ordinary objects in the room and refracted through the lens to produce wondrous and intricate designs. Whether you used a simple homemade tube filled with beads, strings, and paper clips, or a higher-end prism adorned with colored plastic, glass, or marbles, the angled mirrors allowed you to change the view with every twist.

While generations of people have had this experience, no one has ever viewed two identical images. Despite the simplicity of such a low-tech device, it produces an infinite array of beautiful possibilities. We love kaleidoscopes because they combine the beauty of stained-glass windows, the majesty of sunsets, and the surprise of fireworks. The unique design of kaleidoscopes provides new and unusual visual experiences, particularly in environments where darkness and uncertainty surround bright light. While it's disorienting at first, the simple method of combining light and movement in new ways gives the viewer an enhanced field of vision.

Not only that, but kaleidoscopes also serve as connectors that prompt us to see and think differently. Artist Judith Paul put it this way: "The kaleidoscope takes a controlled section of chaos; the mirror system converts it into patterns, and the human mind loves patterns. The right brain wants beauty and art; the left brain wants order. The kaleidoscope is science and art, both."[4] So much more than a child's toy, kaleidoscopes represent that linkage of the left and right brain that serves as a bridge between thinking/feeling and sensing/intuition. They acknowledge the reality in the world around us, but expand our field of view by playfully giving us an endless array of permutations.

Spurred on by our desire to shape the future in an ever-changing world, we developed a systematic approach based on the kaleidoscope to help us anticipate what's next. We call it the Futures Framework and it looks at the ordinary world through a structure that acts like a kaleidoscope, allowing us to see the world in a new and beautiful way. We believe it can help YOU think about the future too.

AN OPPORTUNITY TO SEE THE WORLD DIFFERENTLY

The rest of this book is your opportunity to pick up our kaleidoscope and, with each turn of it, see fresh possibilities for your future. With enough twists, we'll show you how to combine these insights into a clearer vision of the future. We'll then show you, based on that clarity, how to realize that future in a structured, systematic, and actionable way.

Here's what you can expect going forward. In chapter 2, we discuss our shared problem of having limited vision and how we can correct it with futures thinking. We then introduce you in chapter 3 to the four forces that are stirring uncertainty in the world. These forces are continually at work to keep your vision obscured, and we share how recognizing them can help you navigate the chaos around you. In chapter 4, we introduce you to the Futures Framework and use it in chapters 5–12 to teach you how to identify your preferred future. In chapters 13–15, we tie the whole thing together by showing you how to develop an actionable strategy to realize that preferred future.

We were created for vision. Without it, we lose our restraint and our hope (Prov. 29:18). Just as studying history helps us avoid repeating past mistakes, peering into the future from a different perspective unlocks and informs a whole new realm of opportunities. We're confident that as you change your view, your vision will grow. You'll uncover new patterns and see things in entirely new ways; that, in itself, is the first step to creating a different future. Let's get started!

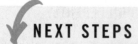

NEXT STEPS

1. Do you have a great memory from when you were a child and were free to play? What stands out to you about it?

2. Have you ever used a kaleidoscope? What did you enjoy about the experience?

3. Are you first drawn to science and order, or art and beauty? How does that influence how you approach your work?

4. Does vision come easily to you? What environments or relationships bring out the vision in your heart?

5. What frontier is still unexplored for you, personally or professionally?

2

INTO THE UNKNOWN

Deep seemed the valleys when we lay between the reeling seas.[1]

—SIR ERNEST SHACKLETON

One of our favorite adventurers is Ernest Shackleton, a polar explorer who led four British expeditions to the Antarctic. Shackleton is best known for his successful failure.

As the story goes, at the turn of the twentieth century, the world was in a polar frenzy. Whoever became the first person to cross the uncharted Arctic landscape was guaranteed unprecedented fame and fortune. It was a time in history now known as the "Heroic Age" of polar exploration when these pioneers set out to conquer desolate and forbidding lands.

Financed by the billionaires of the time, and bolstered by public support, polar exploration was the old-fashioned equivalent of space exploration today. Nations competed with each other, vying to conquer dangerous new frontiers and stake territorial claims. It was also an era of technological advancement and innovation. The tools of exploration included ships designed to brave the unforgiving Arctic ice and capable of withstanding the extreme cold. Even today, a journey across Antarctica is one of the harshest tests a human being can endure.

Shackleton was one of many who aspired to this greatness. In search of scientific knowledge, as well as glory, he set off in 1914 to cross Antarctica from the Weddell Sea to McMurdo Sound in the Ross Sea, via the South Pole. The total distance of the expedition was a formidable 1,800 miles.[2] It was a feat that no other explorer before him had yet accomplished—and for good reason. It was an incredible journey, especially in the early 1900s, and one that challenged all the preconceptions of the time.

Unfortunately, the passage didn't go the way Shackleton planned. He began the voyage with a mission of exploration, but it quickly became a mission of survival. His ship, *The Endurance*, became trapped in an ice floe overnight, surrounded by pinnacles of ice far taller than its sides. He and his crew ultimately abandoned it. His team ended up stranded on Elephant Island, 350 miles further north toward South America, with nearly no hope of rescue. Shackleton became a hero when he led a small party on an unbelievable rescue mission into Chile, ultimately returning four months later to rescue the rest of his crew.

A JOURNEY INTO THE UNKNOWN

You may relate to Ernest Shackleton. As a leader, you also have a weighty responsibility to navigate your team through the chaotic world around you to a better future. You set off on this journey when the sky was blue, when your crew was ready to board, and when you all shared confidence that you were heading in the right direction—but then everything changed. The vessel that was supposed to help you successfully circumnavigate a continent is now frozen solid in the ice. The hurricane-force winds swirling around are unrelenting, and help is nearly a thousand miles away. You aren't even sure how you got yourself into this situation. It all happened so quickly. You know you have to do something, but you just aren't sure what to do.

You aren't alone. As we've worked with leaders of organizations, churches, and ministries to help them navigate the unknown future, we've heard many similar stories. We're usually called right after the ship has been stuck in the ice, and the crew is without hope. What we've found in these situations is that we can all benefit from understanding how, even after the shipwreck, Shackleton continued to defy the odds against him.

Shackleton's journey started as a grand mission of fame, glory, and scientific endeavor. So, if we judge the success of it by these objectives, his mission was a colossal failure. His ship never reached Antarctica, and his crew never set foot on the continent. The expedition strained Shackleton's finances to a breaking point, and the accomplishments he did achieve were eventually eclipsed by the unfolding of World War I shortly after that. Yet if we stop with the failure of his well-planned objectives, we miss something important about Shackleton.

What's truly unique about him is that no matter what challenges he encountered, he continued to envision a better future and went after it unrelentingly. It's unlikely that before Shackleton departed on his journey, he imagined the disasters he would face, but when these setbacks and hardships did occur, he wasn't willing to accept the future that fate tried to hand him.

His commitment to a larger purpose allowed him to see alternatives where others couldn't. Faced with the seemingly impossible, Shackleton was open-minded in the face of enormous adversity. He imagined how his current circumstances could evolve into any number of possibilities over time, and then with unwavering courage and forbearance, he worked to overcome the chaos. When his expedition encountered serious trouble, Shackleton reinvented the crew's goals. Each time the environment changed, and his plans failed, he adjusted. His willingness to persevere through continually changing circumstances helped him get to that better future.

OUR BLURRY VISION

Ernest Shackleton's story could have ended quite differently. He could have suffered from a common condition called *nearsightedness*. Near-sightedness is simply the inability to focus on objects far away. You can think of it as being "shortsighted" or as having "tunnel vision," resulting in the inability to see beyond your present circumstances.

Nearsightedness isn't a new phenomenon. Scripture reminds us that it's been part of the human condition for as long as we've explored our planet. In Deuteronomy, God gave Moses a song to teach the Israelites because He knew they were nearsighted and would forget His faithfulness in the future. The lyrics include, "You were unmindful of the Rock that bore you, and you forgot the God who gave you birth" (Deut. 32:18). And, in 2 Peter, Scripture exhorts us to remember the importance of living out godly characteristics such as self-control and steadfastness. Peter writes, "For whoever lacks these qualities is so nearsighted that he is blind, having forgotten that he was cleansed from his former sins" (2 Peter 1:9).

Another notable example in Scripture where God calls His people to a God-sized future beyond what they can see in front of them is Genesis 12:1–3. Abraham is given a promise that seems impossible: "I will make of you a great nation, and I will bless you and make your name great, so that you will be a blessing. I will bless those who bless you, and him who dishonors you I will curse, and in you all the families of the earth shall be blessed."

Yet after God reveals this promise in chapter 12, we see just three chapters later that Abram is still struggling to have vision for the future that God had promised him. God, in His patience, filled in the picture and invited Abram to believe in a bigger future than he thought possible. The only way he could see a future was to have a male descendant, which Abram didn't have. God told him not to fear or to seek a backup plan, but that he would have offspring that numbered the stars. Abram "believed the LORD, and he counted it to him as righteousness" (Gen. 15:6).

It's so easy for us to have limited vision. We are quick to see only what's in front of our eyes and fail to participate in the promises God has planned for us in the future. Where there's no vision, the people perish, says Proverbs 29:18.

If Shackleton had been nearsighted when his ship became ice-locked, he might have been overcome with the enormity of the challenge ahead of him. Instead of persevering, he may have given up when faced with such an uncertain future. He would have likely failed to adjust his goals or to convince his crew to work together for a common cause. Shackleton's team might have died from cold, famine, and scurvy, as they each worked to preserve their own comfort and safety. And, you wouldn't be reading about him today because his voyage would have been long forgotten as one of many polar tragedies.

If we're honest with ourselves as leaders, we're all more nearsighted than we want to admit. Given the volatile and uncertain world we live in, many of us have difficulty stepping back and gaining perspective. With all of our responsibility to address the urgencies of our present crises, even the most well-intentioned of us are tempted to stop where we are. Instead of envisioning a better future, the immediate goal of managing risk today, improving our resilience, and safeguarding the longevity of our organization, church, or ministry takes precedence. It's easy to maintain the status quo when we're faced with ambiguity and limited resources.

Our blurry vision stems from how we usually think about the future. Since it hasn't happened yet, we don't have an easily accessible framework for our thoughts or feelings about it. When we think about life one day or one week from now, we can generate concrete and specific images. We can predict more details about tomorrow than we can about next year. The reality is, though, "that people tend to think abstractly as they ponder the distant future."[3] The further out we go, the less certainty we have. For example, have you ever been in a job interview where they asked you, "Where do you see yourself in five years?" What would you say? "Feel fulfilled. Be happy. Work less, and play more. Make a difference." It's a standard question that's often hard to answer well.

Yet, most of us want to know what happens next. We're wired for it. Whether it's the next significant development in our industry or the end of a good book we're only halfway through, we want to see the direction before us. We wonder how we will keep up with others who seem to be constantly innovating and how we will navigate the treacherous sea that presents more obstacles with every storm. But since we can't know the future with certainty, we often revert to the one thing we know the best: the past. Learning from the past is critical, but as we recount the mistakes we don't want to repeat, we may unconsciously reinforce the assumptions and biases of our past that keep us there. This can make it hard to move forward. Even more concerning, when we only take our cues from history, we may miss out on the innovations and new approaches that are possible.

A classic example given at almost every talk on innovation is the Eastman Kodak Company. They invented the first digital camera but were unable to see the potential of the growing digital photography revolution beyond the company's core business assumptions. To its ultimate detriment, Kodak was so blinded by its past success and the apparent strength of the status quo that it failed to shift away from film manufacturing and alter its strategy. It's a timeless reminder for all of us that we need to revolutionize our industry before someone, or something, else does.

As we work with leaders, we have yet to talk with one who dreams about a future where their organization closes shop, their ministry goes bankrupt, or their church slowly fades out of existence. No one wants to join Kodak as another victim overcome by the disruptive power of innovation. Instead, all of the leaders we've interacted with have envisioned a better future—and the same is probably true of you. But just because you can imagine it, doesn't mean you necessarily know how to make it happen, especially when your longer-term vision, destination, or outcome meets human limitations, assumptions based on the past, or external factors that inevitably interrupt your course.

You need more than a gut feeling or ethereal sense about where you're heading to lead others into the unknown future. And, while it's not possible to predict the outcome with absolute certainty, not thinking about the future doesn't help either. Within these pages, it's our goal to help you correct your nearsightedness so you get specific about what you want the distant future to look like and, as a result, lead others well.

THE ANTIDOTE TO OUR NEARSIGHTEDNESS

So how can you address your nearsightedness? The solution is straightforward: You need something to shift your perspective and to stretch your visual field to new places. You need a new lens to give you better vision. This is where futures thinking comes in. It's the perfect antidote to nearsightedness and applies to all areas of life, including education, space travel, city planning, or small group ministry.

Do you remember how we talked about kaleidoscopes in the last chapter? Well, futures thinking is like putting on a brand-new pair of kaleidoscope glasses. The approach helps you systematically consider what comes next through a particular set of lenses to foresee a range of possibilities, identify options, plan, and shape the future. The purpose of futures thinking isn't to answer the question of what *will* happen. Instead, its focus is what *could* happen and what that means for your organization, church, or ministry. It can stimulate conversation, widen your understanding of what might be possible, strengthen your leadership, and inform your decision making. Rather than waiting for change to happen to you, it gives you a chance to proactively navigate your reality in the direction you want to go.

Futures thinking is by no means a recent development. It emerged during the Enlightenment, and grew throughout the 1900s with experiments in forecasting and systems operations. Since then, it's become well-established as an academic discipline and a business approach to navigate what lies ahead and develop creative new strategies to reduce uncertainty and lessen the risk of failure.[4] Systems mapping and scenario planning evolved to help leaders like you understand more complex dynamics and create space to consider what seems currently unthinkable.

You can use futures thinking as a way of inspecting your beliefs, habits, and processes. It can help you reveal your assumptions, break free of your constraints, and reevaluate what's possible, even with the limitations of your current policies, practices, and processes. Changing your perspective can reveal gaps between today and tomorrow where you can apply innovation. It can also help you identify the areas where the current successful practices should scale up to have the most significant impact.

Futures thinking allows you to reflect meaningfully on the changes that may occur in the next few decades so you can do something meaningful about them. It's important to remember, though, that you can't know the definitive future; only God knows that with certainty. But you can use discipline and discernment to listen to Him and prompt you along alternative paths. By knowing your God-given identity and purpose, you can have a plumb line that helps you see the possibilities, recognize His voice as you hear it, and keep your navigation accurate in the storm. "The heart of man plans his way, but the LORD establishes his steps" (Prov. 16:9). The goal with futures thinking is not to be right about the specific future but to be prepared for the future because you helped create it.

WHY THE FUTURE IS PLURAL

As we talked about earlier, it's easy to think about the trajectory of any future event in a linear fashion. However, the future rarely emerges predictably. Just think about the stock market, the result of political elections, the latest pandemic, the unfolding of almost any historical event, or the future of the church. Human affairs are neither predictable nor deterministic, no matter how certain they appear at one moment in time. Even though it's tempting to try to anticipate one "correct" future, thinking about the future isn't about being able to define what's going to happen precisely. There isn't just one possible future.

Therefore, when contemplating what's next, it's appropriate to think in terms of "futures"—and that's what futures thinking does. If you took a course on it at a university or attended an online workshop, you would learn a simple construct that includes three key elements: the expected future, the preferred future, and the alternative future.

We can portray any situation or opportunity as having many possible futures. So, these three elements include all of the scenarios we can imagine—some more realistic and probable than others. We can use these approaches as a way to prepare our organization, church, or ministry for change and for us to start to take action.[5] The more we explore various scenarios, the more we can reduce blind spots, minimize risks, and encourage more innovative thinking. So, let's take a closer look at what the expected future, preferred future, and alternative future might include.

THE EXPECTED FUTURE

The future most of us are familiar with is what we call the expected future. It's what comes to mind first and is often based on historical analogy or extrapolation of your current situation. As we all learned in science class as kids, inertia keeps objects moving in the same direction and the same velocity unless acted on by an outside force. Your expected future is the one you will predictably encounter if no external force intervenes.

Consider your life. If nothing were to change in the next five years, what do you expect to happen? You may still live in the same house, on the same street, and be part of the same team, company, and community. You'll likely frequent the same coffee shop, while you drive the same route to and from work. If you are honest about it, this is what you all too often anticipate will happen, right? It's the expected future.

Take the declining rates of church attendance in the United States, especially among young people. An unprecedented number of post-millennial young adults do not identify as Christians. Many consider themselves "nones," and affiliate with "none of the above" religious traditions. We'd expect that in the future, given all we know now, that this would continue.

The expected future is heavily influenced by our expectations, our stereotypes, and our life experience. We tend to resist change naturally, and the longer we persist in the status quo, the harder it is to get out of that status quo. But that's why you're reading this book: you aren't sitting around waiting for the expected future.

THE POSSIBLE FUTURES

Futures thinking requires thinking about more than just the expected future. You also need to examine the full realm of possible futures to identify other unforeseen alternatives.

It's helpful to treat the future as a set of possible outcomes rather than focusing on one specific future that is most probable. To do this, you need to be conscious of the factors that limit your understanding of the future. You have to be aware of your lack of information and what you don't know. Doing this includes considering the possibility of incorrect theories (what each of us thinks we know but don't get right) and unexamined assumptions (what we believe we know but don't reconsider).

As you continue to question, examine, and reconsider your assumptions, you'll discover more possible alternatives. These alternatives may seem more speculative and harder to develop because they're influenced by so many different factors, with varying degrees of plausibility. Developing possible futures is a hard task because of the *unknown unknowns*. These are situations that are so unexpected and unforeseeable that you cannot even conceivably consider them based on experience or your best investigation. Who could have imagined a global pandemic that forced churches, schools, and organizations around the world to challenge their assumptions about gathering digitally, almost overnight? While few anticipated this, it took months to fully appreciate the depth of change caused by this unknown unknown.

One way to anticipate the future in a constantly changing and uncertain world is to develop alternative futures. You can do this quickly by collaborating with people who are different from you. Intentionally bringing together various viewpoints combines the perspectives of people from diverse cultures, backgrounds, and experiences to create something that none of you could have created alone. This type of collaboration allows you to change your vantage point and discover hidden variables that you were unable to see from your earlier perspective.

Although we might not have been able to predict when a global pandemic would occur, we could have proactively envisioned a future where churches met online and didn't require a building. We also could have rethought how we approach missions so that we're planning trips to meet the needs we see in the digital world just as we work to address the needs in a physical world. Rather than wait to be disrupted, we can choose to innovate and be prepared. Shifting our perspective and questioning our assumptions allows us to generate alternative futures that will undoubtedly unlock new possibilities for your organization, church, or ministry.

THE PREFERRED FUTURE

The preferred future is the one that you most desire. It's the vision of a better world that you would like to see and is the end state you're working toward with intention. By using this simple classification, futures thinking helps you imagine potential future scenarios that can help you gain knowledge, understand your situation better, and evaluate information about the future more systematically, to influence it.

When you're clear about your preferred future, it allows you to shift the conversation toward the best way to get there. For example, if we put it in the context of church attendance, the preferred future might be that we prefer that *everyone* attends church and develops a personal relationship with Christ that they live out in community with others. This may not necessarily require meeting in a building, or even gathering in a physical place. Having a vision for what the preferred future could be and mobilizing your organization, church, or ministry to achieve that vision is the fundamental responsibility of all leaders.

You can think about the future on a variety of different scales (global, national, local) and over a range of time frames (near-term, middle-term, distant). If you don't consider what might happen in the future far enough into the future, the results can be too aligned with current trends and tend to support ideas that build within these trends incrementally rather than disrupting them completely.

LOOKING TOWARD HEAVEN

One of the main differences between taking a class in futures think-ing and reading this book is that we offer a gospel-driven framework and consider the future from a Christian worldview. This book is a guide for leaders like you, who are bringing the unchanging gospel to a changing world. As you navigate your organization, congregation, and ministry through this uncertainty, your primary aim is to usher in a future that is aligned with the purpose, vision, and calling God has placed on your heart.

In the Lord's Prayer, we're instructed to pray: "Your kingdom come, your will be done, on earth as it is in heaven" (Matt. 6:10). For all of us who follow Christ, heaven is our preferred future. It's the ultimate destination, the grandest of all possibilities, and the perfect example of the result of futures thinking. We want heaven to be the future that shapes where we're going from where we are now. None of us have been there yet, but we believe that God has given us direction and insight to get past what we can't see with our natural eyes and help us shape our *now* with the promise of *then*.

BECOMING FOCUSED ON THE FUTURE

Walt Disney is well-known for being a visionary leader. His leadership wisdom, "If you can dream it, you can do it," is timeless. The idea for the inimitable theme park we know today as Disneyland was born during family trips with his two kids to local zoos and parks. While his children whirled together on the merry-go-round, Disney spent his time imagining how he could improve the experience. It's said that "his sense of nostalgia for his formative years in the American Midwest, his fascination with the future, and his vision for family entertainment" is what drove him to create a new alternative for people to enjoy.[6]

Great leaders have vision, but there are few natural visionary leaders like Disney. It takes practice to shift your sights away from the obvious, expected future and envision a better alternative. How do you imagine a better ride when the merry-go-round seems entirely sufficient? Being able to define and communicate a preferred future and frame a strategy to get there is a core competency of every great leader. Professors and futurists Peter C. Bishop and Andy Hines explain that those who are most successful in the long term "have mastered the basics of change, how to anticipate it, how to manage uncertainty and ambiguity, and ultimately how to proactively create the changes necessary to bend the future to more preferable outcomes."[7]

Think back to the story of Ernest Shackleton. Among the most critical ingredients in the account of his expedition was his ability to look at his current circumstances with a future-oriented mindset. Disney shared this mentality as he faced a number of significant challenges. He grew up poor and had a difficult family life as a child. He experienced work tensions, lost the rights to his creations at times, and navigated the many ups and downs as he advocated for his work.[8] For each of these men, a future-oriented mindset played a critical role in how they coped with unrelenting challenges. Each of them was able to communicate his preferred future without predicting what was going to happen with certainty. Neither knew all the details, but they were still able to steer others in a prevailing direction, all while overcoming the obstacles ahead of them and weathering the storms around them.

Like Shackleton and Disney, we all need to develop a more future-oriented mindset. We need to be open to envisioning and creating new possibilities so we can help our organizations, churches, and ministries adapt to what's coming, even when we aren't sure what the future holds. We need to answer both the long-term question, "Where do we want to be?" as well as the short-term response to, "What do we do next?"

So, how do you become more like these two leaders? You'll need a disciplined approach to help you focus on specific topics to guide your thinking. Now that we've identified our natural tendency to be nearsighted and the antidote to our blurry vision, in the next chapter we'll teach you how to identify the invisible forces that are swirling around you and causing havoc in the world.

 **NEXT STEPS**

1. Have you ever started a journey and had a surprise change or interruption? How did it impact where you ended up?

2. Why do we say "futures thinking" instead of "future thinking"?

3. Is your mindset more past-oriented or future-oriented? Why?

4. Who is a leader who has modeled resilience and adaptation to change well? What did you see in them that you want to emulate?

5. How would you currently define your expected future, personally or professionally? Can you think of alternatives to the expected future? Are you able to define your preferred future?

3

THE FOUR FORCES

Vision is the art of seeing things invisible.[1]
—JONATHAN SWIFT

Have you ever almost been blown over by the wind on a stormy day? Even if you haven't, you've witnessed the effects of this invisible force in the world in some way. The wind is uncontrollable and often unpredictable. Scripture tells us that it "blows where it wishes" (John 3:8). The wind can cause erosion, launch projectiles, and decimate cities. Its capability is evident in the funnel of a tornado and causes havoc if we aren't prepared. For sailors, the same wind that powers their vessels can also destroy them if not correctly navigated.

With the use of technology, meteorologists can track the wind through interactive maps that help us visualize its effects in insightful ways as it moves around the globe. These maps show how the wind moves across the Earth in real time and are mesmerizing to watch. They allow us to view this phenomenon at a macro level. We can observe with wonder as the wind follows the contours of forests, skims across bodies of water, and sweeps through mountain ranges.

Just as the wind erodes rocks over time, transforming them into new landforms, there are invisible forces that are shaping us, our communities, our organizations, and our churches in significant ways. We are all aware that we live in a world that's rapidly changing. We see the change all around us. The change is organizational, demographic, structural, and technological. But which one of these forces is driving the chaos? There are four key forces at work—and you may be surprised to learn that you're already familiar with each of them.

THE FOUR FORCES

The four forces aren't new. They've been around since the beginning when God intentionally ushered in His creation and order.

In the opening chapters of the book of Genesis, God spoke the earth into being from a void and formed a *place* that He soon filled with good things. His good creation included *people*—first Adam and later Eve—who were made as God's image-bearers in the world. Next, God gave Adam a *purpose* and commanded him to tend to the beautiful garden that He cultivated. Adam now had meaning or a reason to exist and could see his impact as he interacted with the world around him. He began to care for the garden and to classify the creatures, naming and grouping them. Finally, as Adam, Eve, and their descendants began to interact with the world we're commanded to oversee, God gave us the *technology* we need to make sense of and utilize the ever-growing knowledge we gain.

Since the beginning, these four forces—purpose, people, place, and technology—have significantly impacted our history and our future. The weight of their influence remains unchanged to this day. Let's look at each of the four forces a bit closer—and, as we do, imagine them set in a kaleidoscope lens.

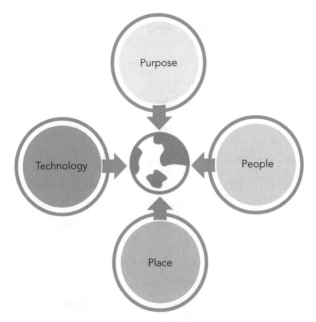

The Four Forces of the Futures Framework

PURPOSE

The first force is purpose: the overriding sense of mission and calling that influences every aspect of our lives. We find purpose in many places, including our families, jobs, churches, and volunteer work. It shapes the why for us, and as our purpose changes and grows, it touches every part of our future.

As Christians, we believe God is the One who gives us each a clear and personal purpose. While this isn't a book about understanding God's purpose for your particular life, we recognize that His purpose is a force that influences our direction, informs our decisions, and guides our thinking.

PEOPLE

The second force is people, encompassing the changing expectations, preferences, and behaviors of humanity, both individually and collectively. Awareness of how the demographics of our communities shift over time is an important consideration for any organization, church, or ministry. Today, this is especially true as the workforce spans five generations. The preferences, practices, and life experiences of each subsequent generation can be quite different.

PLACE

The third force is place. It's the where, when, and how we live, work, and worship. Place matters because it's the foundation for community and connection. It's vital to how we experience others and build something larger than ourselves.

Over time, place has become more fluid in our lives. This shifting includes a change from place being solely physical, to also being digital. It's now quite common for many of us to work from home, have on-the-go meetings, worship in the car while on the road, or co-live with a group of friends in shared housing. Churches meet in coffee shops and houses as much as they meet in 300-year-old brick buildings. Whereas individuals used to frequently stay rooted in the same town they lived in as children, those stories are now the minority.

TECHNOLOGY

The fourth force is technology, which captures the overwhelming and disruptive impact that advances in human ingenuity and creativity have on how we communicate, collaborate, and coordinate at every scale. Technology is the most widely discussed—and most obvious—driver of change.

Fifty years ago, no one owned a personal computer. Now, we not only have desktops, but we also carry computers around in our pockets or wear them like watches on our wrists. We talk to them in our kitchens and our vehicles. In 2001, futurist Ray Kurzweil wrote, "We won't experience 100 years of progress in the 21st century—it will be more like 20,000 years of progress (at today's rate)."[2] Technology has flooded into almost every part of our lives and continues to advance at incredible rates.

EMERGING PATTERNS

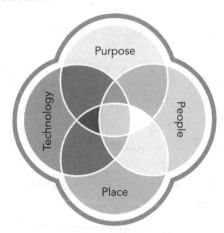

The Futures Framework

The four forces of purpose, people, place, and technology are the core elements of our kaleidoscope approach. We call it the Futures Framework, and it's pictured here. Individually, each force has a measurable influence on the world, but have you ever considered what happens when they're combined?

For example, what does it mean when a younger generation grows up fiercely focused on purpose in a world wholly immersed with technology? What happens to how people develop community online and in virtual worlds? It's not merely one force that's shaping our world, but rather the reality of living under the impact of all of them at once. While each of the four forces presents its challenges and opportunities, it's the interplay of these forces that are most helpful to us in understanding the future.

The Futures Framework allows us to explore the various combinations of these forces and the change they create in the world around us. As each of the forces overlaps with another, intricate patterns are formed at their intersections. We'll talk in more detail about these intersections in the next chapter, but first, let's revisit the story of the polar explorer, Ernest Shackleton, to discover why futures thinking and, ultimately, the Futures Framework, matters.

THE INVISIBLE FORCES SWIRLING AROUND

One of the most amazing moments in Shackleton's Imperial Trans-Antarctic Expedition was his voyage aboard the *James Caird*, a small lifeboat named after the philanthropist who financed the expedition. As you recall, Shackleton's ship, *The Endurance*, was jammed in the ice. He and his crew ended up stranded on Elephant Island, just one day's sail from the nearest whaling station on South Georgia Island. Their only chance of survival was to modify one of their three lifeboats. Shackleton chose the *James Caird* because it was designed to withstand the most chaotic of the seas of the Southern Ocean and, therefore, the most likely to survive the journey.

The rescue party of six set out from Elephant Island. By midnight, the sea started to swell and the winds began to toss the small vessel, undoubtedly giving the crew flashbacks to the loss of *The Endurance*. As the stars in the sky were blotted out by storm clouds, the choppy waters threatened the integrity of the *James Caird*. Since the lifeboat was open to the hurricane conditions around them, the rain constantly pelted their faces like tiny stones making it nearly impossible to see. The waves tilted the ship forty-five degrees, then crashed back into the deep valleys, making it impractical to hold on. At one point, the waves spun the vessel sideways, and it nearly capsized. As Shackleton and his men encountered the worst of the weather, they navigated only on the very brief appearances of the sun.

Imagine yourself in Shackleton's shoes. The invisible force of the wind is swirling around you. Its unrelenting impact on the waves and the rain promises to upend your meager vessel as you try to squeeze through treacherous icebergs closing in on you. What would you do? As leaders, we all feel the impact of invisible forces in our lives, and it's up to us to react or respond. Sometimes we wrongly react when what feels like hurricane-force winds push us in the opposite direction of where we thought we were heading. At other times, we respond strategically to these forces because they feel more like a tailwind, making the path before us effortless. You may be able to think of a specific instance when one of these wind-like situations has happened to you.

No matter what invisible force you face or how it feels, it's up to you to navigate your organization, church, or ministry in the direction of the preferred future you envision. Just like humanity has mastered how to leverage the sun, the wind, and the roaring of a river to create power plants, you too can harness the forces of purpose, people, place, and technology. You can learn how to direct your team and navigate the chaos that these four forces are creating around you.

Like a sailor, who's surrounded by the total darkness from the thick clouds blotting out the moon and stars, your job is to influence the direction of the boat, measure its progress, and adjust the path to keep you moving forward. The forces themselves are neither good nor bad; they're simply a reality that you need to be aware of to navigate well.

When explorers like Shackleton set out on an adventure, they recognize that it's impossible to predict the weather with certainty. All they can do is be prepared for the changes that sudden, potentially violent storms can bring. Shackleton's team survived the two-week journey across 800 miles of stormy seas because he trusted that a better future existed, he used a few simple tools to navigate the life-threatening ocean, and he confidently adapted to the changing conditions. We believe that with futures thinking and, more specifically, with the Futures Framework, you too can navigate your own choppy waters.

A SIMPLE TOOL TO HELP YOU NAVIGATE THE UNKNOWN

We developed the Futures Framework as a proactive, intentional approach to help you benefit from futures thinking to create transformational change. Exploring futures is more than merely an educational exercise or discussion topic that enables leaders to deal with uncertainty. We believe it's critical for your organization, church, or ministry's survival. Throughout the rest of this book, we'll show you how to use the Futures Framework, like a kaleidoscope, to better respond to the four forces causing chaos in your world. We'll use it to help you develop clarity about where you're headed and discover insights on how to navigate in the right direction.

The Futures Framework provides a common language that catalyzes discussion, collaboration, and cooperation. It will assist you in aligning the outcome of futures thinking with your mission, developing an actionable strategy, and scaling your efforts so that you begin to see an impact in your team today. As you use the kaleidoscope of the Futures Framework to explore the patterns that form out of the refracted light, we hope you uncover a new understanding about something that previously seemed ordinary. If done well, you will also find meaningful new actions that you can take to start to work toward your preferred future.

NEXT STEPS

1. Which of the four forces are most influencing your world? Which one seems to have the least impact on your organization?

2. Have you changed physical locations often in your life, or not? How does the sense of place impact you?

3. What's the one piece of technology you can't live without? Why?

4. The most basic question everyone faces in life is: "Why am I here?" Do you know your purpose in life?

5. How do you tend to respond in situations that seem hopeless or don't have a clear answer?

4

THE EIGHT
INTERSECTIONS

Simple can be harder than complex: you have to work hard to get
your thinking clean to make it simple. But it's worth it in the end
because once you get there, you can move mountains.[1]

—STEVE JOBS

In the last few chapters, we've written a lot about kaleidoscopes. It's a toy
we were both fascinated with as children. We each spent hours looking
at the world around us through this magical lens. You may have too.

Think back to when you held a kaleidoscope to your eye, pointed
it at an object in the distance, and then rotated it. For us, the results
were mesmerizing. As the light reflected in different ways, beautiful
patterns emerged. The designs weren't something we could have predicted. Each image was composed of abstract reflections of the light,
and as we continued to rotate it, the images changed. New patterns also
took shape when we re-oriented the entire kaleidoscope in different
directions. Even as the object in our view shifted, without rotating the
kaleidoscope itself, the intersections of color collided and created an
endless array of options.

Now, as adults, we realize that our experience playing with kaleidoscopes taught us that to understand how to better respond to

the forces shaping our world, we need a tool to help us change our perspective. We need a different way of thinking and of seeing, and to recognize that there's always something new to see. Our Futures Framework works in this way. Let's take a closer look at its parts and how it functions.

IT STARTS AT THE EYEPIECE

The critical part of the kaleidoscope—and the Futures Framework—is the eyepiece, which is represented by the outside circles in the following diagram. When you look at the world through the eyepiece, you have an opportunity to reflect on how the four forces of purpose, people, place, and technology collide at each of the intersections. Like a kaleidoscope, when you overlap these four forces and shift your perspective, you not only consider the impacts of the force itself, you also uncover the patterns and insights where two or more of these forces are at work.

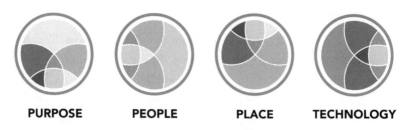

PURPOSE   PEOPLE   PLACE   TECHNOLOGY

The Four Lenses of Purpose, People, Place, and Technology

While you aren't able to see the entire world at once through the eyepiece, what you can do is limit your field of view and focus on an object in the distance. When you do, you examine that particular object more intentionally and explore it differently. You aren't consciously searching for an answer from the object of observation, but rather allowing solutions to emerge from the landscapes exposed by your observations.

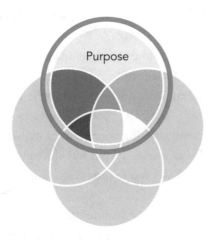

For example, consider how purpose could impact the way someone interacts online. Also, think about how the forces of people and
technology might collide if you focus on how a younger population
uses their mobile devices to interact with each other.

You can point the eyepiece at any combination of issues to generate insights, opportunities, and alternatives to help you rethink your
future, align it with your top priorities, and calibrate it to have an
optimal impact in the changing world. The framework equips you to
identify the key changes you need to make and develop alternative
approaches to help usher in your preferred future. It can be adapted
to any context, whether you're working with refugees on the island
of Lesvos, meeting people online in a virtual gaming environment,
working with government officials in Central Asia, or gathering in a
suburban church in the American South.

If you're systematic in your methodology, you can explore your
future much like an astronomer maps the universe with a telescope.
The universe is much bigger than the limited view of the eyepiece itself.
Just like an astronomer would be unable to map the solar system if
they didn't systematically move the telescope around, you would miss
the bigger picture if you were to look at the future by considering just
one of the forces in sight. If the astronomer assumed that the universe

was only what they saw within the telescope, they'd completely miss the bigger picture.

So, while each of the four eyepiece images is beautiful, on their own, they're still insufficient to help you understand your future. It's not enough to only consider the impact of where technology collides with purpose, people, and place. You also want to examine how the other three images are affecting your plans as well. The combination of all of the insights as you work your way through the entire Futures Framework is what allows you to produce a more complete picture of your preferred future.

Let's be clear: Every force has an influence on the others. Nothing happens without a place, and at least one person. Everything has some sort of purpose and uses technology in one form or another. The intersections in the Futures Framework highlight the specific interactions between the forces that are causing change and uncertainty in the world around us. As you work your way through the entire Futures Framework, you will generate insights by considering each of the individual intersections between the forces.

Interestingly, the kaleidoscope that is the Futures Framework is a time machine bridging the gap between your world today and your preferred future tomorrow. The observation-driven insights, collected over time and from various perspectives, gives you a foundation for new vision. Although only God knows with certainty what tomorrow holds, it's within your ability to envision what a better tomorrow could look like. You can do that by carefully considering the forces driving change today as well as have clarity about who you are, who you connect with, what communities you're a part of, where you gather, what you're designing, who you could collaborate with, how you'll use technology to scale your solution, and what impact you hope to have. Futures thinking makes this possible.

THE FUTURES FRAMEWORK

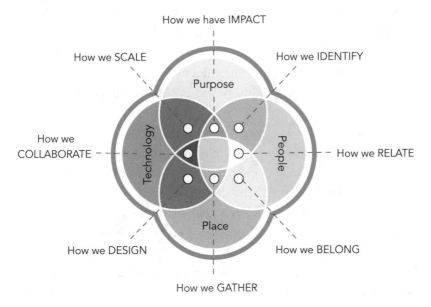

The Eight Intersections in the Futures Framework

The rest of the book focuses on using the Futures Framework to help you develop a preferred future and a strategy to achieve it. In the next eight chapters, we'll help you take stock of your current position. Analyzing the four underlying forces driving the change will help you understand your readiness for the future. We'll pause at each intersection point and consider the theme that results at the collision of the forces.

We'll start with the intersection of the two forces, people and purpose, which results in your *identity*. In our culture, how we self-identify as individuals has never been more vital than today, particularly when it comes to issues of gender, ethnicity, affiliation, and vocation. There are countless quizzes on social media to help you determine everything from your personality type to your perfect vacation location to what prince or princess you are most like. Still, these assessments aren't too helpful in answering the core question at the intersection of people and purpose: "Who am I?"

Next, we'll consider how the addition of place to the people and purpose forces allows you to consider how we *relate* to one another. It didn't take long in the book of Genesis before God created a companion for Adam. Our drive to connect with others is as true today as it was then. We have an innate desire to experience intimate and meaningful relationships with one another. We'll examine how people connect today.

As we work our way around the Futures Framework, we'll explore what it means to *belong* in community with others. Belonging is one of the core needs in Maslow's hierarchy of needs (the well-known psychological theory developed in the 1940s to explain human motivation), following right after physiological and safety needs. Nevertheless, so often, many of us feel as though we don't fit in. What does it take to create and nurture a sense of belonging? Does it require physical proximity? Does it need consistency of communication or meaningful exchanges of support and love? Do you have to give anything up to belong? What does this mean for the isolated elderly in our communities or colleagues in a cross-generational workplace?

Next, we'll explore how communities come together and *gather* at the intersection of people, place, and technology. We'll explore your assumptions about how you currently convene. If you're a pastor, do you need to meet in a physical church building to have a church service? Can you have meaningful, authentic online relationships? How do communities come together? How is the distinction between local and global being redefined in a world where everything's connected?

Having connected with others in community and gathered together in a place, you'll begin to *design* solutions that meet a real need and will ultimately have an impact on your world. As you architect your future, you'll learn how to respond to the forces driving change by having empathy for the user of the solution you're designing. What are the expectations we have as spouses, employees, church members, adults, children, and citizens? What are the approaches to design that you can use to be more effective?

With a solution in mind, we'll consider who else you could *collaborate* with to usher in your preferred future. Collaboration is more than just a simple exchange of information. It happens when two or more people work together toward a common goal. Technology has changed the way we collaborate. We can talk instantly to coworkers on the other side of the world and equally contribute to a task or goal together. We'll consider how technology alone isn't enough and what you can do when you create a culture of collaboration.

Next, we'll consider how technology and purpose can help you amplify and *scale* your vision. We'll explore not only ways to scale but also the barriers that hold you back. How can you invite others to contribute to your purpose, and start a movement using technology, to scale your vision at the intersection of purpose and technology?

After scale, we'll look at how technology, people, and purpose are allowing organizations, churches, and ministries to have *impact* like never before. By connecting communities and initiatives that share a common purpose, you can accomplish previously unimaginable things. The insights and alternative futures generated by the Futures Framework are only useful if they can apply to real challenges you have. After all, the whole point is to have a lasting impact—which is the last of the eight intersections. We'll show you how to tie the future impact you want to have to the mission statement you're working toward today. We'll offer different examples that apply the Futures Framework to everyday challenges.

FROM PREFERRED FUTURE TO LASTING IMPACT

We won't stop there, though. After we consider each of the eight intersections individually, we'll show you how to combine them to gain clarity on your preferred future. We'll also help you develop realistic action plans based on a gospel-centered approach to modern-day challenges in any industry or ministry.

As you read the next section and examine the possibilities ahead of you, you'll need to fight to keep a focus on the future. It's easy to revert to your old assumptions or inherited practices that strangle the innovation out of companies, churches, and ministries today. When the invisible hurricane-force winds are swirling around you, it's easier to do nothing than to do something. You may be the only one on your team taking the time to think about what comes next, so you'll have to help bring others into that process with you.

Along the way, you'll see how easy it is to become indoctrinated by the way you were trained to think or become paralyzed by the habits you were rewarded for continuing. Our intention is to show you how to solve the same old problems in a brand-new way. By focusing on the future, rather than on what could've been done better in the past, you'll start to glimpse entirely new plans God has for you, and uncover innovative ways to get there.

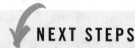 **NEXT STEPS**

1. Do you have any reflective practices in your life that help you gain a new perspective? How did you discover them?

2. Of the eight lenses of the Futures Framework, which interests you most at this point? Why?

3. Of the eight lenses of the Futures Framework, which seems the least relevant to you right now? Why?

4. What tends to distract your attention from the future? How can you stay focused?

5. What issues or challenges are you facing right now that you could use the Futures Framework to help you rethink your future?

PART 2:

THE FUTURES

FRAMEWORK

5

IDENTIFY

Only if your identity is built on God and his love . . .
can you have a self that can venture anything, face anything.[1]

—TIM KELLER

We **identify** in Christ (chapter 5). At the intersection of purpose and place, we explore who we are today and in the future.

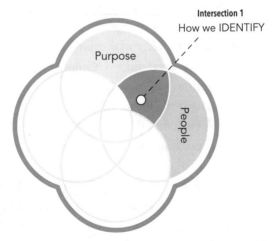

Imagine you're having a conversation with your future self. Across the table from you sits an older—and hopefully, wiser—version of you. What might this future self say about who you've become? Are there qualities that have stayed the same and are still a core part of who you are?

Now, envision from the perspective of this other you that you're living your preferred future. Life has turned out precisely as it should have. However, this doesn't mean it happened the way you currently believe it might. As you listen, would you have predicted with any accuracy all of the changes that occurred? Probably not.

One of the amazing traits of humans is our ability to use mental time travel, as you just did. Our capacity to step forward or backward in time is one of the characteristics that distinguish us from animals. We do this by reliving our previous accomplishments or imagining how we might act in the years to come.

But, this simple mental exercise of talking to your future self points out something important about our ability to project ourselves into the future. Despite our remarkable talent to anticipate what's next, we consistently underestimate the changes ahead, even the changes about how we'll change.

Harvard researcher Dan Gilbert explains that we frequently assume that who we currently are is who we'll be throughout our lives.[2] His studies show that we're terrible at predicting our future selves, which jeopardizes our ability to make wise decisions today. Imagining what the future might be like is far more challenging than staying comfortable in the assumptions and experiences of the past. Essentially, we get stuck thinking that the future will closely resemble today, rather than being able to envision other possibilities. When we change our expectations about our future self, we're able to think differently about what that future self might want or feel.

Our identity—or who we are—is central to everything we do, both today and tomorrow. In the Futures Framework, identity is the first of the eight themes because, without a strong understanding of who you are today, it's hard to determine where you're heading tomorrow. In the framework, identity is located at the intersection of people and purpose, which makes a lot of sense. Identity is uniquely human, and it's tied directly to your purpose. So, when you have a better understanding of your identity, it reveals to you your purpose and your future as well.

WHO DO YOU SAY THAT YOU ARE

Before you read any further, ask yourself this question: "Who am I?" Write down your description, or talk it through with a friend, spouse, or team member. While it may seem like a simple question at first glance, it's often difficult to answer. Identity is complex and multifaceted. It defines who we are and often drives what we do, what we like, where we tell others we're from, and how we see ourselves. Because of this, there are many ways you could describe yourself—and how you respond is often dependent on who's asking.

One way to answer this question is to think about how you introduce yourself to others. Look at these examples:

"Hi! I'm Jake. I'm a corporate executive, a husband, and a father of three."

"Hey, I'm Andy. I live in New York City, and I'm a citizen of the United States."

"Hello, everyone. My name's Sarah, and I'm a child of God."

You might list your activities, interests, or talents. Or, like Jake, you may define yourself by your occupation, role in an organization, or your relationships with others.

Another way to think about how we identify ourselves connects to how we validate who we say we are. On an average day, how many times do you have to provide identification? You may not pull out your birth certificate regularly, but if you pay attention, you'll realize that you're continually asked to confirm your identity.

Passwords are required to log in to your computer, to access your email, and to view your documents. You flash your driver's license at the airport to pass through security and, if you work in a corporate office, you may wave an ID badge to gain access. Two-factor authorization protocols are tying your identity to multiple digital devices at once. There are also ever-increasing layers of fingerprints and facial scans just to unlock your phone. For all of us, our unique biometrics have become our "digital fingerprints." We're increasingly being defined based on our hand geometry, retina patterns, and voice waves.

Unfortunately, our biometric data doesn't thoroughly explain who we are, even in the digital world. Our identity has to do with much more than the biometric parameters of our physical body or how we introduce ourselves. Let's look at identity more closely.

WHO YOU ARE AND WHO WE ARE

Identity is fundamental to our human experience and at the core of human activity. Psychological identity frames how we see ourselves. Legal identity drives how we function in society. Social identity defines how we build relationships and participate in our community. Online identity shapes how we connect in virtual worlds. Our identity influences how we see ourselves today and defines the obligations we embrace that shape tomorrow.

Identity is about you *and* us—all at the same time. It's part of who we are individually, as well as the groups of which we're members. Who you are defines where you fit in and where you don't. It underscores where you belong, where you find power and agency, and where you engage. It guides your strategy, structure, and processes. It influences your reputation and defines how you interact with the world.

These boundaries also create intersections that frame the diverse impacts of the forces of purpose, people, place, and technology. For example, changes in technology might have less of an impact when you're with family but more of an effect in an academic setting. The conversation about purpose intersects one generation differently than it may impact other generations who work on the same team.

As technology develops, though, the public conception of our identity is more persistent than it once was. Who you were at fifteen is in some ways as discoverable as who you are at thirty. Constant connectivity, location services, and social networking create a record of everything. Your identity takes on a shape of its own online as others find posts, pictures, and other pieces of "who you are" perhaps without ever meeting you. These may include what you own, the music you've listened to, any legal infractions you've committed, and even your DNA. You no longer contain your identity solely in your being, but it's externalized and traceable apart from you. Your sense of who you are, which develops as you grow, becomes more rigid because of these persistent artifacts of who you *were*. This externalization of identity can alter how others see you—and how you see yourself.

SPHERES OF IDENTITY: THE PROPHET, PRIEST, AND KING

Identity also extends to our circles of influence, which are often determined not only by the groups we belong to but by the work we do and the offices we hold. When we study the ministry of Jesus, we see a clear example of this.

In the fourth century, a writer named Eusebius of Caesarea found it beneficial to consider who Jesus is through the work He did. Jesus' work can be thought of in three functions or "offices" that He carried out during His earthly ministry: prophet, priest, and king.[3] As Father Philip-Michael F. Tangorra explains, this threefold office is commonly called by its Latin name, the *munus triplex*. A *munus* (singular) signifies a service or a mission one has been sent to do. Tangorra notes that when we talk about Jesus or any Christian leader being a prophet, priest, and king, this means we aren't merely implying that they hold these offices. We're also saying that they do this type of work, pursue this type of mission, and have this type of impact.[4]

While many throughout the stories of Scripture have held these various offices, only Jesus perfectly fills all three roles simultaneously. He's the true Prophet, Priest, and King. Let's explore each of these offices separately and briefly look at how Jesus fills each one.

A prophet is, as Tangorra describes, "one who teaches others the way they should live, so as to avoid evil and embrace the good."[5] In the Bible, we see prophets—such as Samuel, Elijah, Isaiah, and Haggai—as the ones who spoke and taught on behalf of God. A prophet is committed to listening to God and sharing what God is speaking to him with others. During Jesus' earthly ministry, He consistently communicated the Father's heart for people in word and action.

Priests offer sacrifices on behalf of others and intercede for them. Scripture tells us that they represented humankind before God, "standing in the gap" for the people.[6] In the Old Testament, Aaron and Eli both filled the role of the high priest, but when Jesus came and died, He became the final and perfect sacrifice. Hebrews 4:14 calls Him "a great high priest who has passed through the heavens," and in Romans 8:34, the apostle Paul tells us Jesus now sits at the right hand of God interceding for us.

A king is someone who rules over or governs a group of people. Kings use their power to protect a kingdom and build its wealth, as well as ensure—as Tangorra notes—that those they govern reach their full potential.[7] They hold ultimate authority and are due all allegiance in their particular realm. In Scripture, kings included David and Solomon. Jesus' kingship is different, though. While the Israelites waited for a king who would defeat Caesar, Jesus' kingdom isn't of this world . . . and of that kingdom, "there will be no end" (Isa. 9:7).

Eusebius's categorization of Jesus as prophet, priest, and king has been used by the church throughout history as a helpful way to describe who Jesus is and the purpose of His ministry. This *munus triplex* has also helped reveal important truths to us about God and how we can relate to Him. Understanding how Jesus connects to the Father and communicates His heart—even when that might be difficult to hear—compels us to respond to what He says. Recognizing how Jesus stands before God on our behalf and intercedes for us even now, reminds us of His faithfulness and our security. Honoring Jesus as king requires that we acknowledge His authority and invites us to trust His protection. Only as we learn to relate to God for who He is can we discover who we are.

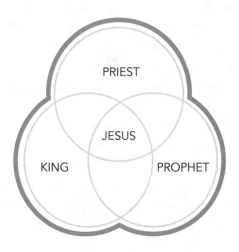

THE ENTREPRENEUR, THE PASTOR, AND THE EXECUTIVE

How does the *munus triplex* apply to us as we examine identity? More specifically, what does it have to do with who you are—both today and in the future?

Before we explore this, it's important to note that not everyone finds Eusebius's categorization helpful. When it comes to the modern-day application of it, some criticize that these offices pigeonhole leaders into restrictive and unhelpful categories. For example, it's argued that kingship in the Old Testament has more to do with covenant faithfulness than with organizational leadership, and that "prophets weren't primarily teachers or expositors of written revelation." Instead, "they were recipients of direct divine revelation."[8] For our purposes, though, we're not seeking to offer a leadership typology, but rather, to look at the continuum of callings we can apply in our context. We're using the threefold offices of Jesus to represent universal patterns of human nature, the overlap of roles and identities, and how they can help us define our spheres in new ways.

For example, a prophet can be thought of as an entrepreneur. Although entrepreneurship is often attributed to starting a business and scaling it for profit, the true core of entrepreneurship is about transforming the world by solving the big problems. Entrepreneurs carry a vision that others may not quite see yet. They imagine the world differently and spend a lot of their time communicating this vision to others.

Similarly, a priest can be compared to a modern-day pastor. Pastors have an overwhelmingly large job description. They're shepherds of the church, they're teachers, they're caregivers, they administer sacraments, and they're ambassadors to their community. While different from the Levitical priests referenced in the Bible, pastors "stand in the gap" to help connect people with God.

Finally, a king can be thought of as an executive. An executive is anyone with managerial responsibility in an organization or ministry. They could have great titles such as Chief Executive Officer (CEO), Chief Information Officer (CIO), or Chief Financial Officer (CFO). Just like the role of a king in the Bible, or in countries that still have kings today, an executive occupies a position of authority over people and resources.

Do you see how these offices go beyond spiritual gifts or church roles and may drive your identity in other spheres? We'll use these three examples as models throughout the book to apply the Futures Framework to several settings, such as starting a new ministry venture, leading a local church, or guiding a company.

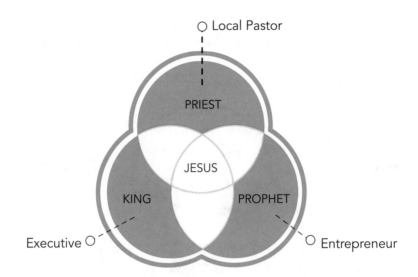

THE FORWARD-LEANING EXECUTIVE, THE MEGACHURCH PASTOR, AND THE CHURCH PLANTER

You may not associate perfectly with the different stories as we represent them throughout the next seven chapters—and that's okay. What if you're not a traditional executive in your organization, but see yourself as more of a forward-leaning, innovative leader, that just happens to have an executive-ish sounding title? Or what if you're technically a pastor, but you actually spend the majority of your time running a megachurch and therefore connect much more with books written for CEOs of corporations? And what are we to make of a church planter, who is essentially an entrepreneur, without the venture funding?

We encourage you to use the examples as inspiration for your own situation to celebrate the unique overlaps you see in your life. A key insight of this book is that the most interesting futures occur at the intersections of the forces driving change in our world. This is also true when it comes to roles we hold in the organizations, churches, and ministries. We no longer live in a world where we strictly define our work responsibilities by the title on an organizational chart. You can draw ideas from any one of the examples, or go in a completely different direction as you refine your identity, define your preferred future, and impart realism based on actual examples and experiences.

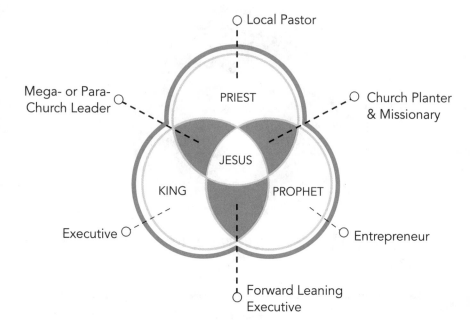

THE AS-IS STATE

Remember how, earlier in this chapter, we asked you to describe who you are? Hopefully, you either wrote it down or talked about it with someone you trust. If you didn't, we encourage you to pause now and take some time to do it. The strongest leaders are the ones who are clear about who they are, what they do, and how they do it. Most of them start by assessing who and where they currently are. Now that we've closely looked at identity, that's where you can begin too.

As you start applying futures thinking to your organization, church, or ministry, it's useful to develop a baseline of who you are as an individual and a leader today. You can do this by understanding and describing your current situation.

Let's think about this in terms of a timeline between now and a set date in the future. With this timeline in mind, describe the status quo. How do things exist today? We call this the "as-is" state. It's the present state or who you are now, which also includes your organization, church, or ministry's current vision and values, strategy and mission, products and services, process and systems, structure and approach, opportunities and challenges, and community and culture. Describing your as-is state is a critical first step that provides a starting point for the more difficult work of futures thinking ahead. It also, as we've mentioned, implicates your history because that's a piece inherent in your present.

Once you have your as-is state defined, the next step is to envision who you'll become as a leader. If you could describe your future self on the other side of the table, what would be the same and what would be different? What's working and what isn't? Imagine drawing a straight line between who you are today and who you anticipate you'll be in the future.

Next, consider what the world would look like if you're able to attain that future state. Would the lives of every person in your community look different? Would there be no more poverty? What needs would be met? You likely have a mission statement and a vision statement for where you want to lead your organization, church, or ministry. How are you doing at actually fulfilling it, or would anyone notice if your organization didn't exist? Once you have a description of who you are in the future, you're able to more specifically think through the variables that would have to change from today's status quo to make this future a reality.

11 PERCENT SURVIVAL RATE

It'd be easiest to continue what you're doing now and expect a future that's simply extrapolated from the past and projected into the future. Unfortunately, as we've discussed, that's not how life works. Just as Shackleton's polar exploration didn't go as planned, there will likely be unforeseen events that disrupt your organization, church, or ministry at any time. It's highly likely that no matter how well you describe your future self, when you get to that moment in time, the reality will be different.

This is what's happened to many former Fortune 500 companies in the United States. In the 1950s, our space program had just been formed. Our country was about to embark on an adventure to win the space race and put a man on the moon. The same year that NASA was founded, companies such as American Motors, Brown Shoe, Studebaker, Collins Radio, Detroit Steel, Zenith Electronics, and National Sugar Refining were on the Fortune 500 list. They were some of the most powerful and successful companies at the time. Today, NASA is the anomaly. It's still in business, but fewer than 11 percent of the Fortune 500 companies in 1955 have remained on the list.[9] Will the titans of today, such as Walmart, Apple, Exxon Mobil, Facebook, Google, Microsoft, Home Depot, and Target still appear on the list in 2078?

These Fortune 500 companies remind us why defining a preferred future version of ourselves isn't enough. We also need to be open to other alternatives. There are many possible alternatives and a broad set of possible futures. Our challenge is we're limited by our ability to identify them and our capacity to prepare for them. However, if you analyze the world you operate in and are attuned to both current changes and ones likely to occur in the future, you might come up with a few alternative futures within the realm of possibility given your organization, church, or ministry's recognized strengths and constraints.

WHAT MATTERS—AND WHAT DOESN'T

There's a story told that when Michelangelo sculpted his famous statue of David, he could already "see" the man hidden in the block of stone. His key strategy was to decide what didn't belong. "'It is already there,' he noted. 'I just have to chisel away the superfluous material.'"[10] Identity is in many ways as much about deciding what matters and what's superfluous.

The culture values one set of principles while the church encourages another. The online world honors even more diverse standards. We can run after the superficial pursuits applauded by media, culture, and society, which have no real lasting or satisfying meaning. We've both worked in large—and often bureaucratic—institutions and have seen how easy it is for negative beliefs to slip in unknowingly. We've experienced how assumptions about who we are can limit our ability to move forward. It's easy to act like everything matters—or like nothing does.

So, what can you do? You can reframe your future with a solid foundation in the reality of how God sees you. When you became a Christian, you became a new person. Your value is based on your relationship with Jesus, and your identity stems from who He says you are. When you know—and accept—who you are and your unique God-given purpose, then you can start to define where you belong in the community and in the world. Understanding and articulating that value and uniqueness is essential to identifying your potential futures.

Who you are and who you aren't, along with who you want to become, is the fundamental intersection of people and purpose. How you understand and articulate those truths define your possible and preferred futures. As you come to appreciate that, you gain a perspective within which you can relate to others in your community.

So, it's time to continue identifying who you are. Think back to how you described your as-is state and your future self earlier in the chapter. If you still aren't sure at this point how to describe your identity, list all of the roles and titles that you have on your team or in your community. Write your thoughts down because we'll build on this over the next seven chapters. You can jot it down on the Future Canvas worksheet in the back of this book or download the worksheet at futuresframework.com.

NEXT STEPS

1. As a child, what influenced who you thought you were? As an adult, how has that changed?

2. How do you talk about your identity as an individual? In your community? In your organization?

3. What do you communicate about who you are with how you present yourself, personally or organizationally? Personally, this could be in what you wear, where you live, or how you spend your time. Organizationally, it could be your logo, your uniform, or how your office is structured.

4. Do you connect more with the exhorting role of the prophet, the shepherding role of the priest, or the governing role of the king? We all take on these various roles at different times. Does one of them feel particularly aligned with how you're made?

5. Are there places you feel like your identity is challenged or questioned? As a parent or spouse, as a company, or as a believer? Who or what causes that challenge?

6

$$\boxed{\text{RELATE}}$$

Carve your name on hearts and not on marble.[1]
—CHARLES SPURGEON

We identify in Christ (chapter 5) and then **relate** to others (chapter 6). At the intersection of purpose, people, and place, we explore how we can connect with people in new ways.

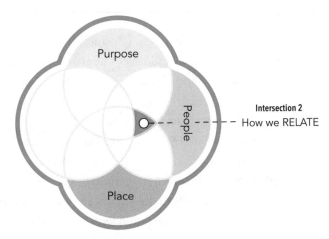

In 1972, inspired by the Space Race, chronobiology pioneer Michel Siffre decided to explore what happens to humans who isolate themselves from connection. He descended 440 feet into Midnight Cave near Del Rio, Texas, and stayed there, confined to a platform, for six months.[2]

Siffre saw no people, no natural light, and no calendars or clocks. He completely disconnected himself from his normal rhythms and the community with whom he identified.[3]

- By day 37, his sleep/wake cycle shifted radically. He lived through an extremely long day and then slept for 15 hours.

- By day 77, his hands no longer had the ability to string beads, and he could "barely string [together] thoughts."[4]

- By day 79, feeling on edge, he called his team and asked to leave the cave. They encouraged him to stay.

- On day 160, he saw a mouse. Desperate for company and connection, he began to look for ways to trap it.

- On day 170, he accidentally killed the mouse and was left in despair.

When Siffre emerged from his isolation on day 180, he reflected on his learnings and what it might mean for future space travelers. The sensory deprivation and lack of human companionship had permanently changed him. By the end, he had become "a half-crazed disjointed marionette."[5]

Historically, psychologists, researchers, and church leaders almost unanimously agree that living in isolation isn't healthy. While for most of us, it's indeed possible to "survive" for short durations of time without human interaction, it's not a condition—as Siffre's story and likely our own experiences illustrate—that we're able to endure long term. We're social beings and interaction with others appears to be essential to our growth, development, and well-being. We quickly fall apart outside of relationship.

CREATED FOR RELATIONSHIP BUT LOST IN LONELINESS

A few years ago, we worked with Syrian refugees who flooded into the Greek Islands. They were fleeing from their war-torn homeland where they had no hope to provide for their families, their sons could be conscripted at any time, and their daughters might be assaulted or trafficked. In search of a better life and security, they fled across the Mediterranean Sea, mostly on rickety rafts. Families arrived by the dozens in overloaded rubber boats, their every possession stuffed in bags and backpacks. Parents clutched the hands of frightened, wide-eyed children who didn't speak a word of Greek or English.

As boat after boat of refugees unloaded, our focus was to get them warm and dry. As we brought the refugees into the camp, the first thing they asked for was an internet connection and a charging station. Before they showered, were provided with tents, or even ate, they wanted to connect with their family and friends. Letting their loved ones know they were alive, sharing photos of their journey, or just talking with them, was more urgent than eating or sleeping. They had a desire, a drive, and a need to re-establish the links to the people and places from where they came. Without this, it was too difficult for them to cope with being in a foreign land. Connecting with their family and friends meant that they could still be themselves—that they could be human.

Our experience with the Syrian refugees taught us this: how we relate with others is essential for survival. It has been since the beginning of time. Relationship is something we do because of how God made us unique as humans.

Do you remember in chapter 3 how we talked about God creating humans as His image-bearers in the world? God Himself exists as an eternal relationship between the Father, Son, and Holy Spirit. He doesn't dwell in isolation, and He didn't design us to either. In this most fundamental way, we reflect the image of God. He intentionally fashioned us to be in relationship with Himself and with one another. He wired us to desire meaningful ways to connect.

It's interesting that the first thing God called "not good" was being alone (Gen. 2:18). Before God addressed the loneliness Adam felt, He paraded representatives of the animal kingdom before him. As Adam named each animal, he discovered the basic truth that it was impossible to truly connect with any of them. They weren't like him. None of the animals completely saw, understood, or corresponded to his humanness. Aware of Adam's isolation, the Creator caused him to fall into a deep sleep. Taking a "rib," God carefully and artfully molded a suitable companion: woman.

Just like Adam and the refugees in Greece, we too desire to relate to others—physically, spiritually, and emotionally. We're made for relationship, and it's good . . . until it isn't. Whether it's a broken marriage, a family member who's become distant, or a close friendship that's faded away, we've all experienced isolation. Despite our God-given need for connection, we don't always embrace authentic relationship or navigate it well. Our sin has rendered us perpetual relationship breakers who—like Adam and Eve after they sinned—hide when we feel exposed and vulnerable. Because of this, we often trade actual relationship for a shallow connection.

Most of us know isolation is a problem in society, and maybe even in our lives. We realize that we weren't created to exist in solitude. But how can we stop hiding and embrace the possibilities of being seen and known? What makes an authentic and lasting connection possible?

THE CURE FOR LONELINESS

In her book *Frientimacy*, author Shasta Nelson notes that authentic relationships require three things: positivity, consistency, and vulnerability. Positivity makes the relationship satisfying, consistency makes it safe and reliable, and vulnerability builds a deeper and more genuine connection.[6] When we're missing one or more of those elements, we find ourselves with unsustainable or unsatisfying relationships. So, how do we experience connections characterized by all three of these qualities?

We start by reminding ourselves of who we are in Christ. In chapter 5, we talked about how our value is based on our relationship with Jesus. Our identity stems from who He says we are. We've been raised with Christ (Col. 3:1), which means the old life of brokenness and emptiness has been buried with Him. We're now called to set our hearts on things above (Col. 3:2).

Yet, sometimes we hide from God and others because we forget who we are in Christ. We lose sight of our identity and, as a result, struggle to create meaningful connections with others. But our ability to relate goes hand-in-hand with who we say we are. When we understand our identity, it changes our activity.

We see this clearly in Colossians 3:12–13. These verses tell us that because we're chosen by God, we should put on "compassionate hearts, kindness, humility, meekness, and patience, bearing with one another, and if one has a complaint against another, forgiving each other." This passage describes what it looks like to live without hiding from one another. We can't do these things when we're isolated or have constructed barriers in our relationships.

Each of the relational commands from Scripture requires the three qualities Nelson writes about: positivity, consistency, and vulnerability. For many of us, vulnerability feels the riskiest of the three. As leaders, we often believe it's antithetical to the "strength" it takes to lead. In reality, however, vulnerability is one of the first strengths we need to be an effective leader. When we practice it—along with positivity and consistency—we create authentic relationships.

Now, the truth is that simply because a relationship is authentic, doesn't make it easy. Authenticity is hard. Even though we've been made new in Christ, we still live in a broken world. We all have real lives and real limits, which makes positivity a struggle for us at times. Sometimes it's easy to focus on each other's negative qualities and use those as excuses to unfollow or unfriend rather than faithfully extend forgiveness. Where there are people, there are problems, which is why the consistency Nelson mentions matters. For relationships to last, we have to offer others a safe and reliable connection characterized by biblical compassion, kindness, humility, patience, and forgiveness.

IN CLOSE PROXIMITY

How does our need for relationship tie into the Futures Framework? As we discussed in the last chapter, your identity is located at the intersection of the people and purpose forces in the Futures Framework. Once you identify who you are and what your purpose is, you have an innate desire to connect in relationship. Relating to others is a function of people and purpose.

You may notice as you look at the Futures Framework, though, that how you connect also requires the third force, place. To meaningfully and purposefully relate to others involves proximity. So, let's take a closer look at what proximity is and how technology has impacted how place is defined in our world.

We don't use the word *proximity* much in today's vocabulary. It means closeness and describes something near in space or time.[7] If you grew up in a more analog world, most of your relationships started because of physical proximity. Your ability to connect in meaningful ways with others outside of your immediate physical space was limited. You related to those who lived near you, attended your school, or participated in some activity with you. Your best friends were those with whom you spent the most in-person time.

But, as our world becomes more digitally connected, place has less to do with geographic proximity and more to do with access to technology. More than five billion of the eight billion of us on Earth[8] are now connected through fifty-billion devices.[9] An interconnected global spiderweb of fiber-optic cables connects continents across the seafloor, and satellites connect cities across the sky. Billions of digital devices can constantly send and receive signals giving us all unprecedented, instant access to one another. As a result, families are more mobile, and careers are more diverse. Our behaviors, expectations, and preferences when it comes to where we find relationships are changing in this digital age, especially in younger generations who have more information and options than any who came before them. The advancement of technology offers us the potential to relate to others in simple yet powerful ways. For our refugee friends, it allowed them to connect with their families and friends who were thousands of miles away. Similarly, digital spaces offer us opportunities to interact with family, friends, and coworkers. We see their pictures, hear their voices, and can talk and work together. Our online relationships can be just as real as our offline relationships, if we bring our true selves to these digital spaces.

But these connections we have in digital spaces are only real insofar as they represent us deeply and authentically—and, for many of us, they don't. As a result, we've started to become disconnected from each other without even knowing it.

THE CONNECTION DISCONNECTION

Recent breakthroughs in neuroscience confirm that our brains need connection. When two people are in conversation, they stimulate each other's neural networks within the brain. Author Matthew D. Lieberman, in his book *Social*, says that these neural networks serve to strengthen our social connections allowing us to feel social pain and pleasure, empathize with others, absorb cultural values, and connect to our social groups.[10] We're literally hardwired for connection.

So what happens when we're disconnected? Psychologists explain that in a world where we try to relate with others by "sharing" personal moments online with "friends," replace business meetings with digital "hangouts," or communicate through 280 characters or less, they observe patterns of what they call the "connection disconnection."[11] We're connected without being in authentic relationships. We end up stuck in a pattern of isolation, which technology only makes worse.

Living in a digital world amplifies our inclination to seclude ourselves or to hold up false identities. Take a moment to think about social media. Many people have thousands of virtual followers but no "middle-of-the-night, no-matter-what-people," as author Shauna Niequist calls loyal, real-life friends.[12] They receive online "likes" regularly, but they feel anything but liked. They've isolated themselves in a two-dimensional virtual world that reflects a form without substance, an image that's disconnected from feelings.

As we invest our time in online interactions, our face-to-face social connections are dissolving. In her article in *The Atlantic,* Emily Esfahani Smith explains, "We volunteer less. We entertain guests at our homes less. We are getting married less. We are having fewer children. And we have fewer and fewer close friends with whom we'd share the intimate details of our lives. We are increasingly denying our social nature, and paying a price for it. Over the same period of time that social isolation has increased, our levels of happiness have gone down, while rates of suicide and depression have multiplied."[13]

But it doesn't have to be this way. As a leader you can develop authentic relationships and redefine the future through your connections.

REDEFINING THE FUTURE THROUGH YOUR CONNECTIONS

The Futures Framework starts with identity and relationship because these two themes are fundamental to any future toward which you're working. Without knowing who you are and recognizing your need to live in relationship, your work is futile. You are a ship aimlessly sailing in a vast ocean. It'll be difficult for you to influence others to pursue a higher purpose.

Sadly, many leaders skip over these first two steps and jump right into developing strategies, or worse yet, implementing plans. But when you take the time to build a solid foundation, based on identity and how you relate to others, you'll find that it's an antidote to loneliness. It provides the necessary context for the future work of your organization, church, or ministry. It permeates the way you make decisions, and influences where and how you live, work, and worship.

Your relationship with others—the link you share with them—is what makes any preferred future possible. These connections can be physical or digital (you share a defined space). They can be external (you share a hair color, a neighborhood, or a college major), or biological (you share a bloodline or family history). It's possible they're ideological (you hold a common belief) or experiential (you've been through a similar experience). Some of the links may be more profound than others, and some more static. But every connection counts. It's how you show up to those relationships—or, in other words, the authenticity you bring to them—that determines how significant they can be for you.

Finding that unique connection to the people on your team or in your congregation is critical to your work as a leader. But it's becoming more difficult in the swift pace of our society to do so. As all of our schedules grow fuller, the fast work of life makes the slow work of relating harder. You face the challenge of making a relationship as easy as possible, but simultaneously keeping it as authentic as possible.

As you're developing your preferred future, it's essential first to answer the question of which relationships are key to that future. The diversity of interest and involvement that those around you have makes relationship a question of prioritization. So start thinking about with whom you need to be spending more time.

CONNECTIONS THAT MATTER

Once you've determined which relationships are your priority, the next step is to develop them. Relationships add enormous value to your future. As you engage others, the links you form give your future the direction and meaning it needs. Connections with others allow your vision to become bigger than yourself and your limitations. So, what are some practical ways you can make these connections rich and meaningful? Let's look at four ideas.

Build Empathy

Empathy is the foundation of connection. IDEO's Human-Centred Design Toolkit describes it as a "deep understanding of the problems and realities of the people you are designing for."[14] Empathy drives an other-centered focus that a self-centered connection can never produce. While you may not be able to actually experience what another person goes through, empathy allows you to set aside your preconceptions and see the world from their perspective. The connections created by empathy often become the ones that matter the most and have the greatest impact on your future.

Building empathy starts with listening. Choosing to hear what others are saying—and responding with the same level of authenticity—creates an atmosphere of openness that allows that connection to happen. When you initiate this with people you otherwise might never connect with, and ask them questions about their values and experiences, it's invaluable. It allows you to stand up then and be a voice on behalf of those who might not be able to speak up for themselves.

Get Offline More Often

When you spend time offline with others, it helps you build a foundation to be even more authentic when you're online together. As we discussed earlier, relating to others is hard work. Our culture's push to network instead of genuinely connect only makes it harder. Authentic relationships require taking the time to pause, have a conversation, and get to know someone—and often, you'll need to take time offline with them to do that.

One way you can get offline more is to take a periodic digital Sabbath. When you intentionally step away from social media and devices, it helps you combat dependency and digital addiction. It assists you in fighting the need to be always available, always responding, and always "on." Time offline forces you to remember how to create value and tell stories, rather than depend on a bottomless list of content served up on demand. Additionally, it helps you face your "real life" and not be tempted to escape into an always-available virtual world. As a result, it brings a richness to your life and relationships.

Move into New Places

Our time with the Syrian refugees—and the empathy we gained for them—expanded our understanding of the world. When Michel Siffre emerged from his isolation, he was changed by the relationships he formed and re-formed. Similarly, relationships allow you to explore new places and spaces, which allow you to move into new futures. Every time you add relationships or take them away, new possible futures emerge.

Travel is the easiest way to discover new places and try on new cultural settings. Exploring new communities, joining new teams, trying new restaurants, benchmarking with other companies—they all create relationships and possibilities.

Develop a Shared Purpose

Finding a shared purpose makes connections come alive. It won't be the same purpose with everyone. Some people you'll share theology with; others you'll share history with. There will be those you have small things in common with, and others with whom you share significant interests and experiences. That's okay. It all depends on the part they have in your preferred future and what's essential for them in that role. What you'll need to do is help curate multiple communities with different values. As a leader, you'll have to go slow and create space for uniqueness, valuing effectiveness over efficiency. Relationally, you'll need to be willing to get messy with people.

Developing a shared purpose starts with establishing a mission that's in line with your values. Sometimes this already exists, but it needs clearer language or more specific roles. The key to that shared purpose isn't just purpose *for* (the goal itself) but purpose *with*. Starbucks can't serve great coffee without customers. Radio stations can't be successful without listeners. The disciples had a clear mandate that came in the example of their Teacher. Clarifying and communicating that purpose also clarifies where those key relationships are.

Pursuing and developing authentic relationships with others is a vital, core component of the good work you're doing as a leader in your organization, church, or ministry. When you take the time to prioritize and deepen these connections, they'll help to keep you grounded for the future. So, take a moment now to determine with whom you need to connect. Write it down on your Future Canvas worksheet because we'll continue to build on this over the next six chapters.

 NEXT STEPS

1. Who are the people you're in a relationship with today? Can you define your audience or others whom you serve through your organization? Can you identify those who serve you?

2. How often do you intentionally get offline? During that time, what do you do instead? What can you change to allow you to take a digital Sabbath?

3. How can you connect with people in new ways? What's holding you back now from connecting with others?

4. Where do the people in your organization go to connect with others? How are they currently getting their physiological, safety, and emotional needs met? Where else could they (and do they) go to get their relational needs met?

5. If relationships require positivity, consistency, and vulnerability, in which are you mostly investing your time and energy? Where do you need to invest more?

BELONG

I have come home at last! This is my real country!
I belong here. This is the land I have been looking for all my life,
though I never knew it till now.[1]

—C. S. LEWIS

We identify in Christ (chapter 5), relate to others (chapter 6), and **belong** in community (chapter 7). At the intersection of people and place, we explore how the way we belong is changing.

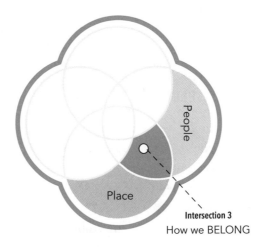

Intersection 3
How we BELONG

At the San Ysidro Port of Entry—the busiest border crossing in the Western Hemisphere[2]—a giant granite monument marks the border separating the United States and Mexico. Between 1849 and 1857, fifty-two marble monuments were erected along the US-Mexican border to mark the boundary. With time, even more were added. By 1894, there were 258 monuments along the almost 2,000-mile border.[3] The monuments proclaim the sovereignty of each nation, and the boundary between them defines the edge of where one country ends and another begins. For some, these monuments represent the future, and for others, it's a reminder of the past.

Boundaries like these are used to protect and defend, but they're also used to separate and divide across the same geographic, ethnic, and political lines. They often define the stories we tell about ourselves and the places we think we belong. Sometimes these stories change.

Recently Ali was exploring her parents' attic with her young niece, and she discovered her childhood globe. Spinning it around, her niece noticed the Soviet Union, Yugoslavia, and West and East Germany and asked Ali about these countries she'd never heard of. As they talked, she was amazed by the idea that each of the country's nationalities—which are defined by their borders—had changed over time. The borders seemed fixed to her even though they are actually fluid. To understand just how fluid national borders are, it's helpful to think about it from the perspective of an astronaut orbiting the earth.

THE ORBITAL PERSPECTIVE

Flying at 17,500 miles per hour around the earth, astronauts have taken millions of photos documenting our beautiful planet. Their pictures show the continents divided only by expansive bodies of water. When you look at these photos of Earth from space, it's impossible to see the lines on a map that separate us.

While these artificial lines aren't visible from space, the world's divided by millions of them. Geographically, boundaries separate the different regions of the earth. Some follow natural features of the earth's surface, like the Alps separate France and Italy, or the Bosphorus separates Anatolia from Thrace. Still others are built or drawn by humans, like Hadrian's Wall that marked the northern edge of the Roman Empire or the 38th parallel that separates North from South Korea. Politically, these lines divide our countries, states, provinces, counties, and cities—and often, the geographic boundaries influence these. Linguistically, these lines differentiate between people based on the various languages they speak. In India alone, there are 122 spoken languages. Economic boundaries isolate people by their income or wealth level. Social boundaries like race, gender, faith, profession, and physical abilities deny some people equal access to resources, creating inequality.[4]

Historically, boundaries have been used to show who's in and who's out, or what's mine and what's yours. They're one way we as humans stake a claim for ourselves and denote our territory in both politics and economics. While all of these lines have reasons for existence, we often use these distinctions to divide or exclude, forgetting that our commonalities are stronger than our differences.

Our friend and astronaut Ron Garan knows firsthand what it's like to view the world from space. Upon returning from his trip to the International Space Station, he explained what he calls the orbital perspective.[5] When he looked at the earth from space, he was faced with a sobering contradiction. On the one hand, he could clearly see the indescribable beauty of the earth with no borders between countries or peoples. His unique vantage point allowed him to recognize we all belong to one planet. On the other hand, he realized the up-close, harsh reality of life for a significant portion of our fractured planet's inhabitants. Nearly a billion people don't have access to clean water, countless go to bed hungry every night, and many die from preventable and curable diseases.[6]

What's astonishing is that we currently have the resources and technology to overcome almost all of the challenges our planet faces. We could provide clean water to all, feed the hungry, and prevent curable diseases. Many argue that the challenge isn't a resource problem; it's a distribution problem. A primary barrier is often the national and economic borders within which an individual is born. Without the borders that prevent us from working together, it seems possible to end wars, eradicate violence, and eliminate poverty from the face of the earth. But the only possible path to get there is, as Ron did, to recognize we all belong to one human race—and the problems of some humans are the problems of us all.

What if we determined that these human-drawn boundaries didn't divide us as much as we thought? Would there still be immigrants or refugees if we eliminated border guards, barbed wire, passport control, fences, and walls? Would the problems of poverty and violence overlap in a way that compelled us all to take collective action? Do we really need boundaries to define where we live, where we attend church or school, or with whom we're friends? As more people view the world from a global or "orbital" perspective, many are asking questions about what would happen if boundaries are redrawn, redefined, and reconsidered.

FROM THE TUNDRA OF NORTH DAKOTA AND THE PLAINS OF TEXAS

Now's a good time to tell you a little more about us. We were born on opposite ends of the United States. Nick is from the cold wind-swept tundra of North Dakota, while Ali is from the humid, swampy plains of South Texas. Neither of our birthplaces can be spotted from space—at least not without the help of high-powered optical lenses—and most people wouldn't be able to pick out our hometowns on a map. But it was our love for exploration that caused us both to leave our homelands, cross borders, and relocate to a new place. More than ten years ago, we were both attracted to a passionate community of curious people who wanted to dare mighty things together.

Our journey is no different than that of millions of people across the globe. Our lives epitomize the increased mobility associated with today's global citizens. We're part of a cultural era that's more ethnically, racially, and cognitively diverse than any time in history. We can now belong to more communities, in more places, with more people. As a result, many of us are redefining boundaries and reconsidering what it means to belong.

While it may have once been the case to have only one job, one hometown, and one steady group of friends your entire lifetime, that's no longer the world many of us live in. More and more people have multiple jobs and live in numerous cities throughout their careers. Millions now define themselves as global citizens first and national citizens second, affiliating less with where they live geographically, who they associate with politically, or how they're categorized linguistically or economically. What brings many of us together is the desire to take on the systemic global challenges of our time as part of a worldwide community committed to lasting change. And it's this sense of belonging that gives us a way to create a better future together.

WHAT IT MEANS TO BELONG

In the last chapter, we talked about how God intentionally designed us to be in relationship with Himself and with one another. Just as we're wired to connect with others, we also have an innate desire to belong in a community. This is why determining where we belong is the third step in the Futures Framework after we identify in Christ and develop relationships with others. In our leadership roles, our ability to belong—and help others do the same—is a powerful way to empower and motivate our workforce, promote diversity, and achieve more effective results.

To belong means to be accepted as a member or part of a community. Belonging is a universal human need, just like our need for food and shelter. In Maslow's hierarchy of needs, the need to belong bridges the gap between the foundational physiological/safety needs and the higher-level esteem/self-actualization needs.

In the Futures Framework, belonging is located at the intersection of the two forces of people and place. You find a place to belong once you find people with whom to belong. Some of us find belonging in a church or with our friends and family. Others of us discover it within our organizations or on social media. There are those of us who connect with a small group of people, while others of us feel a connection with people from around the world.

As Christians, we belong to a worldwide community of those who've been redeemed by the work of Jesus Christ—called the universal church. It's a faith community that transcends ethnic, cultural, and racial lines, and "is the single most important institution on earth, the organism through which God advances his kingdom."[7] Yet, just because we understand the need to belong, doesn't mean we know what it takes to belong. For many of us, even in the church, belonging can be hard.

WHAT IT TAKES TO BELONG

Imagine that you've relocated across the country. You're interested in belonging to a church in your new city. You determine the time and place where this global community (sometimes called the big-C Church) meets locally (the little-c church). It's Sunday morning, and you decide to attend a church service there for the very first time.

As you walk in, everyone seems cheerfully locked in conversation with one another, but they're only speaking to people they already know. Nobody greets you, or even acknowledges your presence. Despite the amazing message and the stirring worship music, you aren't invited into a relationship with others. You shake it off, try once more next week, but it happens again. You probably wouldn't keep coming for too much longer.

Even if you're currently a pastor, you might still relate to this example. After all, there was a time in your life when you weren't in church leadership—and maybe you found yourself struggling back then to feel welcome in a specific congregation. No matter what your current leadership role is, we've all experienced what it's like to feel as if we don't belong. We've all had situations where we can't figure out how to fit in with the people or the place at least once in our life. (In fact, if you haven't felt like this, we'd be worried that you're secretly a robot.)

Belonging is unique in that our mere existence within a specific group of people or in a particular place doesn't necessitate our belonging. Just because we're born in North Dakota or Texas, doesn't mean we belong to either one of those places by default. If someone visits a church on a Sunday morning, it doesn't mean they will feel like they belong to the congregation. There are countless stories of people who don't believe they belong to the family they're born into or the community in which they live. So what does it take to belong?

Often what unlocks our feeling of belonging is shared experiences. These experiences require a community of people to belong to and a place to come together. The place doesn't necessarily have to be a physical location—it could be digital—but it needs to be a spot where we find tolerance, respect, and cohesion with others who share similar hobbies, interests, passions, or goals. If a newcomer to a group feels like there's either a real or perceived impermeable boundary, or that they can't see an easy path to become an accepted member of the community, they'll often give up and leave.

Fostering a sense of belonging isn't the sole responsibility of those who are already established in a group, though. It also requires effort from those new to the community. Think back to the example we gave you of attending a new church. If you're new to a congregation, for instance, creating common experiences requires work on your part as well. You may be tempted to walk in, sit in the back row, wait for others to talk to you, and then walk out without ever sharing your name— much less a real relationship. But what if, instead of waiting for others to approach you, you decide to check out a welcome lunch the church has or join their new members' class? Regardless of the situation, if you intentionally choose not to engage others, feeling like you belong will be a challenge everywhere you go. However, if you decide to initiate, you may be surprised at the belonging you'll find.

SEEING THROUGH THE EYES OF OTHERS

If creating space for belonging is necessary for your preferred future—and, let us spoil the ending, it is—then you need to be able to see your organization, church, or ministry with an unbiased perspective, as an outsider does. In this area, your success in using the Futures Framework depends on your willingness to impartially consider how others perceive your community, and what within it does and doesn't help those you lead to experience a sense of belonging.

For instance, have you created a place that invites and welcomes people with different experiences and expectations? Do they have to read your website to know what you stand for, or are your values communicated in the way that you live? Do people feel that you're for them? Do their individual and unique beliefs and dreams find a place in your community? If so, they're likely to come in—and stay.

One organization we worked with decided to meet virtually anytime two or more were gathered. Place didn't limit who could show up and participate. If one person was virtual, they were all virtual. This way, everyone who belonged to the community was treated equally. A cohort of megachurches we're part of began planting small, hyper-local gatherings in communities, creating places where more people could be known and it would be harder to hide. Another startup developed an online app where congregants could follow along on their phones and tie into reminders via a Bible app. Instead of assuming Bible knowledge and church experience, they were inclusive and not condescending, making a way for everyone to access the content in the way that worked for them.

So, how can you, as a leader, also start to see through the eyes of others? We encourage you to assess three things honestly:

1. How you welcome people.

2. How you represent your own values and respect those of others.

3. How you help people within your community fulfill their dreams and goals.

As you do, remember that shaping your preferred future requires letting go of your assumptions and traditions.

Also, we encourage you to talk to members of your community about how they experience belonging—or how they don't. Remember that you recognize a tree by its fruit (Matt. 7:16). Can you see evidence of belonging among the people you lead? Sometimes you have to give a little feedback to get some, so start by sharing your perspective. Ask both those who are in your target audience, as well as those who are more on the margins. Repeat back to people what you hear from them, and don't get defensive about what they say. You just might see with new eyes.

BELONGING, BELIEF, AND THE FUTURE

In our chaotic, fast-paced, and changing world, belonging is a critical step that most people need to take *before* they're willing or able to believe in something and behave accordingly. To belong and to believe are both active and courageous choices to be authentically present with others. They both require decisions. The difference is that for many, belonging is an easier step than believing.

By its very definition, choosing to belong requires committing. When you're a member of a gym, you commit to paying a monthly or yearly membership fee for the benefit of access to the facility and the staff. When you're a member of a sports team, you commit to showing up every day to practice, to assume a role on the team, and to strive together for a common goal.

Belonging to something also requires that you choose to give other things up. It's a choice that comes with a cost. To get the most out of your gym membership, you may need to give up sleeping in late every day. To belong to a sports team, you may have to choose to submit to the leadership of the coach who'll undoubtedly ask you to do things you may not want to do—such as running sprints or lifting weights.

So, what are the boundaries of belonging in your community?

What does it cost you to belong to the communities that you do? What is it requiring others to belong to yours—and is it worth it?

We often seek belonging before we can believe in a better future. But, once you and those you lead have chosen to belong, you're usually ready to believe. Take a moment now to define how you'll belong or how you'll create a place for others to belong. Note the possible barriers to belonging. Write these things down on your Future Canvas worksheet because we'll continue to build on these over the next five chapters.

NEXT STEPS

1. What significant experiences in your life have taught you about belonging? How are they still influencing your view of belonging?

2. What does it mean to belong to your organization, church, or ministry? Is it hard or easy? What are the criteria for belonging?

3. In your organization, church, or ministry, or with the people you serve, what's the order of belong/believe/behave?

4. Who are the people who don't belong to your community? What can you learn from their perspective on you and what you do?

5. What happens to a society or a community when we decide that everyone belongs? In your organization, church, or ministry, which boundaries are real and important, and which seem artificial or superfluous?

8

GATHER

The church is constituted as a new people who have
been gathered from the nations to remind the world that we
are in fact one people. Gathering, therefore, is . . . the foretaste
of the unity of the communion of the saints.[1]

—STANLEY HAUERWAS

We identify in Christ (chapter 5), relate to others (chapter 6), and belong in community (chapter 7) so that we can **gather** together (chapter 8). At the intersection of people, place, and technology, we explore how the way we gather is changing.

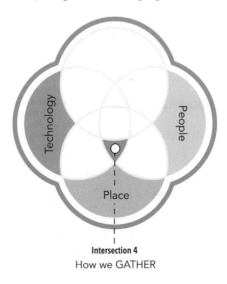

Intersection 4
How we GATHER

In 1597, a Dutch poet wrote the hymn, "We Gather Together," to celebrate the defeat of an oppressive Spanish king.[2] The victory was important for the Dutch people because, up until that time, the king had prohibited gathering to worship. The desire to come together was so strong that the people rebelled. At the Battle of Turnhout, in a town in what's now the Netherlands, 4,000 Spanish soldiers and 500 horsemen were killed. Nearly 5 percent of the Spanish army was utterly wiped out.

After the victory, the Dutch settlers emigrated to America. For many of them, it became the place where the oppressed gathered. To celebrate their independence and remind themselves of their freedoms, the Dutch pilgrims regularly assembled to sing "We Gather Together." The hymn concludes with a fitting plea, "O Lord, make us free!"

This 400-year-old hymn is still popular today and is sung in churches across North America every year on the Sunday before Thanksgiving. In many hymnals, it's the first song in the book.

Although most of us don't face oppression like the Dutch under Spanish rule, this hymn is still a potent reminder of the importance of gathering. The folksy melody and stirring lyrics remind us that God instructs us throughout the Bible—as those who find our identity in Christ—to gather together in relationship with others. In Matthew 18:20, Jesus teaches us the fundamental reason for gathering: "Where two or three are gathered in my name, there am I among them."

RELATIONSHIP AND PROXIMITY

It's impossible to relate with others and belong in community without some kind of ability to gather. Gathering reminds us that life is best lived with others, and requires the key components of relationship and proximity. These two forces of people and place drive how we come together within our communities.

Successful leaders understand the importance of relationship and proximity to gathering. While remote work is a trend that's on the rise, many executives and other marketplace leaders still prefer to meet in offices with their workforce when given the choice. Gathering in this analog way provides teams with an opportunity to be in close physical proximity and further develop their relationship with one another. They interact, generate ideas, and the work gets done.

Churches work similarly. Pastors invite the community to gather on the weekends with their congregations in church buildings. The word *congregation* literally means a group that gathers for worship.[3] Until recently the idea of gathering in a physical building has been so ingrained in our culture that it's historically been easy to unintentionally get caught up in assuming that the "church" is the building, instead of the people inside of it.

Place and people have always been the driving forces of how gathering happens. Until about thirty years ago, we mostly convened locally based on who was closest to us in proximity. Our location, or our geography, was the primary limiter to how we belonged in communities. Without the technology we have now, it just wasn't feasible to think of gathering in any other way. But how we come together is changing, and the speed with which it's happening is unrelenting.

The fourth force of technology has been quietly shifting our world and opening up an entirely new frontier. No longer are we gathering in only analog ways. We're now experiencing a transition to a more digital world. Today, gathering isn't just local; it's also global. Technology creates a bridge where virtual places and digital spaces can connect people in ways never before possible.

THE NEW DIGITAL FRONTIER IS CAUSING SOME PROBLEMS

Digital places are just as real as analog ones. The cameras in our smartphones, tablets, and computers instantly beam us into online experiences with others. Long-distance phone calls have been replaced by chat apps and video calls that immediately connect us to almost anywhere in the world (and even in outer space). Multiplayer games enable us to compete or collaborate in real-time with friends, even if they aren't sitting across the table from us. These digital places have created new frontiers for us to gather, engage, and respond to one another. And, as we're able to connect with people located all across the globe, our world becomes smaller.

For many, the church has already become less about a physical building, and more in line with the biblical definition of a community of believers gathered together to worship. As we mentioned earlier, Jesus Himself defined the church as what happens wherever two or three are gathered in His name. Notice that He didn't specify a location. Gathering could happen in a traditional church building, a coffee shop, or a home. It could equally be online, in a virtual reality app, or through video chat on your device. It might be on a mission together, anywhere in the world. Soon, we may even be able to gather in space, on another planet. We're living in an era where the gathering of the church is known more by its fruit (Matt. 7:18–20) than its location.

Unfortunately, as the forces in the world are disrupting the way we traditionally gather, it's also causing problems along the way. For leaders who prefer an all-analog world, being forced to gather digitally due to forces outside their control, such as a global pandemic, can be disorienting. Many easily use the phrase "the church is not a building," but putting this into practice through a world of connected digital devices is much more challenging. Pastors and their teams feel ill-equipped and under-resourced but have started to consider possibilities of worshiping together and connecting through small groups online. Yet they are naturally asking if it's possible to truly experience authentic relationships in this new digital world. The struggle in the corporate world is not much different. Many leaders are cautiously redefining what it means to be at work when an increasing percentage of their workforce is working remotely. Some are questioning if their teams even need to work in an office anymore to be successful but are struggling with how that will impact the way work has always been done in their industry.

You may have similar questions and reservations about gathering in a digital world. That's completely normal and you're not crazy. But let's talk about it.

THE ELEPHANT IN THE ROOM

Up until this point in the book, we haven't addressed the elephant in the room. So, here it is: *humans don't like change.* No matter how much we say we don't mind it, we actually don't like it at all. We aren't making it up—science confirms it. In fact, we were going to give you a list of sources, but we didn't want to exhaust you. Plus, you can just look it up.

If we're honest, we're afraid. We fear uncertainty and the unknown. It's safer to rely on what's previously made us successful, rather than take a chance on the future. Often, this fear is what keeps most of us from taking action. It tells us that change is dangerous, and we believe this lie is keeping us safe. We want to know what's going to happen before it happens and what it's going to mean for us.

As consultants, we've seen it over and over again. Fear is normal and common. We all have it. Some of us are just better at recognizing when we're afraid, and working through it, than others. It happens so often when we're working with our clients that we've identified three main fears to be aware of when it comes to gathering differently. They're the fear of losing control, the fear of inauthentic experiences, and the fear of not being supported.

THE FEARS THAT ARE HOLDING US ALL BACK

Recently we talked to Lauren, a client who's accountable for a large workforce, an even larger budget, and an overwhelmingly large mission. She admitted that her biggest reservation about their future was her team's desire to gather differently. They wanted to work remotely, and some of them wanted to do so permanently. For Lauren, it felt like a departure from her management style and how they've always done business. "What if I can't meet with my colleagues, employees, customers, and community directly?" she mused. By directly, she meant, "in person, in my office, whenever I want to."

Our conversation revealed that Lauren's core fear was the inability to hold her workforce accountable if she couldn't see them physically accomplishing their work. She was deeply committed to accountability and valued face-to-face conversations, which made her afraid of losing control. It was difficult for Lauren to envision how to fulfill her responsibility and accomplish their mission if they weren't all physically in one place. Her fears came true shortly after, when her workforce was forced to work remotely for months at a time.

Similarly, in a conversation with a pastor named Tim, we asked him why he was hesitant to encourage meeting in virtual small groups. His primary concern was that they wouldn't experience an authentic community. Yet people regularly approached him with a desire to participate in weekly small groups, but for various and entirely legitimate reasons, they were unable to join any of the existing ones. Single parents struggled to arrange childcare, or find time with all of their other responsibilities to travel across town to meet for an hour one day a week. It'd be easier for them to open up a laptop or power up a cell phone and gather online. Working professionals had a similar challenge, especially when they traveled out of town frequently for work. They were free in the evening during the normal time the small group met, but it wasn't possible to be physically present.

We've worked with several small entrepreneurial firms, too, who all had great ideas about how to move their business to online platforms where they could more effectively reach their audiences. Yet we sensed reluctance. The changes went against conventional wisdom. These online places were unproven, and there were no historical trends or metrics to compare against. No one knew for certain what would happen if such a big shift was made. They knew the old places weren't working anymore, but they were afraid of new places because they feared the unknown. One of these entrepreneurs was Aaron. He had a desire to use digital missions to reach the unchurched nones from around the world, but fear was holding him back.

REACTING OUT OF FEAR

Fear is powerful, but it's not the actual problem. The problem is how we react to fear. It keeps us from responding with wisdom and truth to a better future ahead of us. Fear paralyzes us, and we're unable to see alternative solutions. Although it really shouldn't take a global pandemic for us to think about how we could gather digitally, we often wait until a crisis happens to us before we take action. We have been conditioned to unconsciously react to external stimuli rather than thoughtfully respond to what comes next.

So how can you address your fears about the future? Maybe it's helpful to think about what would happen if you don't make a change. As the saying goes, "If you keep doing what you've always done, you'll keep getting what you've always gotten." It's a risky business. Mostly you risk the chance to grow, to do something more, and to create space for God to do more in and through you. By not making a change, you potentially ignore the plan God has in store for you.

It almost sounds silly writing this, but sometimes identifying your fear about the future—the thing that's holding you back—is as simple as writing it down. When you identify it, you're able to appreciate better how you're reacting out of it. Now's a great time to pause for a moment. Put down this book and write it down. What's your fear about the future? How are you reacting to that fear?

If you aren't sure, look back at Lauren the executive, Tim the pastor, and Aaron the entrepreneur. Although Lauren wanted to effectively and efficiently complete the work, she was reacting to her fear of losing control. Tim wanted to worship together in community, yet he was reacting out of the fear that authentic community wasn't possible online. Aaron wanted to unlock opportunities to use technology to reach the unchurched, yet he was reacting to the fear of pioneering an entirely new digital frontier.

Their fears of losing control, unauthentic community, and of pioneering the unknown are three fears many leaders have about the future. Maybe they're even the fears you wrote down. It's likely the reaction to your fears—whatever they are—is the very thing holding you back from envisioning a better future. No matter what you fear, by identifying it and heightening your awareness to the reaction it's causing, you can start to think differently about the future—just like these leaders we've been telling you about did.

With a little help, they each saw how they'd been reacting out of fear and how those fears were holding them back from a better future. They recognized that the shift from analog to digital was creating new possibilities in how they gathered. Each of them decided to jump in and invite others to gather with them in new ways. Lauren saw an opportunity to use remote options to provide more flexibility and work-life balance for her teams. By rethinking how small groups gathered, Tim recognized an opportunity to use virtual groups to connect with congregants in his local church. Aaron identified a chance to use the latest technology to connect with nones globally through digital missions.

Now it's your turn. How will you gather differently now that you are facing your fear of the future? Based on the work you've already done in the previous chapters to identify in Christ, connect with others in relationship, and belong in community, where can you use digital technology to rethink the way you gather? Maybe it's a buildingless company, a remote meeting, an online church, or digital evangelism. Write down your ideas on your Future Canvas worksheet because we'll continue to build on them in the next four chapters.

PRACTICE, PRACTICE, AND MORE PRACTICE

Ultimately, your success in using the Futures Framework not only depends on your willingness to spot how you're currently reacting out of fear but also your openness to try new approaches. The best way to learn something is to practice, practice, and practice some more. To practice, we encourage you to do three things: create new places to gather, be the first to jump in, and then invite others to join you there.

Create New Places

Digital placemaking is as easy as opening your laptop and clicking a button. You have access to technology that you can use right now. It might be tempting to focus on physical spaces and set off on a multi-year journey to build a new building, but we encourage you to experiment first by creating a digital space. It may be much less expensive, and you will likely find that you can reach more people.

If you don't know where to start, identify a place where you currently gather. Ask those who regularly assemble with you if there are reasons they don't come more often or would prefer not to attend more often. For example, working professionals would come to church more, but they're out of town on business travel. How can you create a way for them to participate in the worship experience while they're away? By paying attention to how those you connect in relationship with and belong in community with live, work, and play, you'll discover a host of places to reimagine and reinvent.

Be the First to Jump In

Once you've created your digital space, be the first to jump in. It's tempting to delegate the task of creating and gathering in the space to someone else on your team. Resist the urge! When you express your support for gathering in new ways, by participating yourself, other people notice and will follow your lead.

When executives like Lauren resist the urge to drive to the office, stay at home and encourage everyone else to also, and then open up their computers to connect with an all-digital team, it gets noticed. When pastors such as Tim not only promote the use of technology to meet together weekly but then join the online small group to participate, it gets noticed. When entrepreneurs like Aaron visit existing digital spaces where nones may gather, whether they're massively multiplayer online games, social-media conversations, or virtual reality, it gets noticed.

Invite Others to Join You

The third and final step is to invite others to join you in your new space. This invitation might be as simple as setting up an "asynchronous staff meeting" and asking everyone to post their weekly status updates between 8:00 and 9:00 a.m. on Monday, instead of meeting together in person. Not only will they be happy to gather with you online, but they'll also be thankful you gave them back a precious hour of their day.

IT'S NOT JUST DIGITAL (THE PURPOSE OF TECHNOLOGY)

We've used digital places as our primary example here for two reasons: they're becoming more prevalent in our experience as leaders, and they're accessible to us all. Anyone can create a digital gathering space or join one. But technology isn't confined to online spaces.

When we use the word *technology*, we're referring to the practical application of knowledge to solve problems more quickly or do work more effectively. Remember in chapter 3, how we talked about Adam, Eve, and their descendants interacting with the world? Back then—long before computers and the internet were created—God provided the technology they needed to make sense of and utilize the ever-growing knowledge they gained. Technology is the effort applied to tools to create value regardless of where our story plays out in history. And today, it's a force that's revolutionizing how we gather not only digitally, but also in person. Technology is creating many new possibilities for the time we spend face-to-face and shoulder to shoulder.

One of the key places where we see those new possibilities emerge is through hackathons. A hackathon (a combination of the words "hack" and "marathon") is an event in which computer programmers, developers, and technologists join others from diverse fields—such as graphic designers, interface experts, and project managers—to collaborate intensively on real-world projects. These are exceptional opportunities for hands-on, creative problem-solving of difficult challenges. Global hackathons, or "mass collaborations," take this opportunity to another level by using technology to scale the participation of an international community around a common vision to meet common needs both in their communities and around the world, at the same time.

A few years ago, we worked with a hackathon team in Nepal. Their focus was on how to teach robotics to schoolchildren in one of the least developed countries in the world.[4] At the time, teaching these kids to code seemed a stretch, but they recognized that teaching logic strings and problem-solving were the real fundamental skills that preceded the ability to program. So, they built a low-cost prototype, a digital interface that allowed users to define the logic, and a curriculum that they could apply in the classroom setting. In doing so, they created a whole new experience to which the kids responded wildly. The team recognized that what worked in Austin and Denver didn't necessarily work in Kathmandu. They were willing to think differently and didn't let the lack of access to robotics hardware hold them back. Instead, they solved the problem with the technology they had available and provided an experience that impacted the whole community.

Your community might still gather in person but use different means to get there. The best solution always considers the needs of the users. Whether it's stay-at-home moms looking for community, believers in foreign countries forbidden to gather publicly, work teams collaborating remotely, or international hackathon communities working with small organizations that lack in-house talent, each considers the needs of the users and creates a way to gather that is effective and relevant.

Take a moment to think about how you might gather differently in the future. As you consider this, try not to assume that everyone currently has equal access to technology, or that putting it online will automatically attract a particular age group. Write down your insights on your Future Canvas worksheet and we'll continue to build on this over the next four chapters.

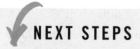

NEXT STEPS

1. What do you fear the most when it comes to the future of your organization, church, or ministry? How have you reacted based on this fear in the past?

2. What's successful about the gatherings you're having right now with your team or community? What seems to be lacking?

3. What can you do to create new places for your community to gather in?

4. How can you create more authentic experiences when you gather with others? How can you reimagine the way you gather for the people you lead or influence?

5. What's required for those you work with when it comes to accountability? Does this change in the future when more people work remotely or in alternative locations? Do you feel like you're losing control? How can you solve this?

9

DESIGN

You cannot predict the future, but you can create it.[1]

—PETER DRUCKER

We identify in Christ (chapter 5), relate to others (chapter 6), and belong in community (chapter 7) so that we can gather together (chapter 8) to **design** solutions (chapter 9). At the intersection of place and technology, we explore new ways to design solutions for a better future.

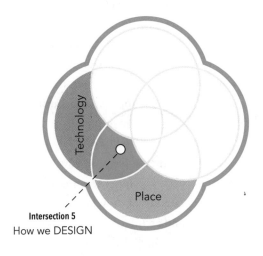

Intersection 5
How we DESIGN

Late on a Friday night halfway through his undergraduate engineering degree, Nick was regretting his decision to sign up for an optional class in advanced thermodynamics. While all of his nonengineering classmates enjoyed more recreational activities, he tried to understand the classical Tsiolkovskiy thrust equation. This eighteenth-century physics and math equation serves as the basic building block of twenty-first-century space mission design.

At the beginning of the semester, Nick was lured in by the course description that promised he'd learn how to design a rocket if he just applied enough effort and discipline (yes, he's a big nerd). But after eighty hours and his sixteenth unsuccessful attempt at solving the problem, he started to understand something even more important than Tsiolkovskiy's formula of aviation. Nick realized that design is hard . . . really hard. More than just understanding ideas and equations, designing solutions—especially new solutions that nobody had thought of before—takes a lot of ingenuity and effort.

Have you ever designed anything entirely new and unique? If so, you know firsthand that the design and development of anything new, whether it's a new product, approach, or system, is really difficult. We've all experienced this throughout our lives. It's far easier to copy someone else or work from an equation than to develop the equation itself. We might understand how the equation works or how the rocket flies, but to design it from scratch requires real ingenuity.

Coincidentally, the word *engineer* comes from the same Latin root as the word *ingenious*, implying the application of mind or intellect. Engineers, architects, and designers are all taught to proactively design new solutions. They apply a specific, repeatable process to create value—and ideally beauty—as they solve problems.

While the construction of a skyscraper requires the hard work of thousands of people, only a handful of individuals contribute early in the process. These engineers and architects are those who know how to approach a complex and uncertain world through the lens of design. Without them, we wouldn't have the Eiffel Tower, automobiles, or the International Space Station. The solutions they develop enhance the standard of living and improve the quality of life on Earth (and in space) for everyone.

The design process taught in school is underpinned by the scientific method. This process-based approach allows engineers and architects to wade through the chaos, ask questions, see a better future, and build a solution that meets their users' core needs. It's actually pretty simple—nothing like rocket science! It starts with identifying the need, followed by developing and testing possible solutions, before finally evaluating the results and iterating if needed.

You may not be an engineer or architect, but as a leader, the design process can work for you as well, no matter what problem you're attempting to solve. Later in this chapter, we'll share three common process-based design approaches that you can use to help you design solutions for your preferred future. But, first, let's talk about what you want and why you want it.

STARTING WITH CLARITY

In the last chapter, we discussed how to identify the fears you're reacting to as the world changes. You discovered that you can recognize the risk of not thinking differently about the future when you identify the underlying fear that's holding you back. But identifying the anxiety that may be driving your current reaction is only half the equation. It's helpful in thinking about your past and how you got to where you are today, but it's less useful in pinpointing where you want to go.

Do you remember how, in chapter 2, we talked about how the future is a set of possibilities, a variety of plausible outcomes that could occur? Well, you can influence which of these possibilities comes to pass, and the best way to influence those futures toward your preferred future is vision. The clarity of that vision is what gives you the means to design the future.

To develop that vision, you need to recognize what you really want and how you might respond in a different way to achieve it. You have to acknowledge your fears, be self-aware of your motivations, and acknowledge what needs you're trying to meet—in yourself, on your team, and with your work. Most of all, you have to be willing to dream big and take the risk. You may be driven by a desire to create change, but to do that, you have to know what you want to change and why it matters. This clarity drives how the process works. Designing a better solution for the future starts with knowing what you want.

So, how do you know what you want? You might have to ask some hard questions such as:

What do you care about the most? What are you willing to fight for?

What are you dissatisfied with? Why is it not working for you?

What do you see around you that others aren't seeing?

What matters for you to work on? Why do you want to work on it?

There's an infinite number of answers to these questions, but here are some possibilities to start with:

I want to help the church respond to my generation.

I want to experience and build authentic community.

I want my team to fulfill its potential.

I want to pivot my business to have more impact.

I want to help missions be more effective.

I want to help foster social/racial/economic reconciliation.

I want to use media to tell a different story.

Those are the *what.* How do we get to the *why?* Here are the whys behind those examples, which are all true stories from our work.

I want to help the church respond to my generation . . . because they matter! And for whatever reason, it feels like the church isn't hearing or understanding the cultural experience of people my age. I want to share my story to help the response be more effective.

I want to experience and build authentic community . . . because I think there's more than one way to do it. I've seen it. And maybe if we all come together with those new ideas, we'll end up with a new result and leaders will see what's possible.

I want my team to fulfill its potential . . . because I'm charged with leading them, and that means I want to serve their dreams, not just have them serve my agenda. I know that our vision and goal has to be more than just the immediate situation.

I want to pivot my business to have more impact . . . because we've been doing something great for several generations, in fact, we're the best at what we do. But the future is different, and we realize we have to do something new as technology changes how we work.

I want to help missions be more effective . . . because sharing the gospel matters so much, but I see so many people coming back home, or struggling for funding, or just trying to build a Western model in other parts of the world. There has to be a better way.

I want to help foster social/racial/economic reconciliation . . . because God desires it, and it isn't happening. Crossing those boundaries is complex, and building that sense of belonging is a challenge. I want to be part of that.

I want to use media to tell a different story . . . because media is powerful! And maybe because we don't like what the current story says. Content is king, and people consume more media than ever before in history. Changing the story will change how people see their future, what they think is possible.

So what do you want and why? If you know, we encourage you to write it down, as specifically as possible. But, for many of us, it's not that simple. Why is it such a challenge to know what we want? Often because it's easier to do what others tell us to do or base our decisions on culture and tradition instead of operating with purpose and intentionality.

Knowing what you want is half the battle. It helps you identify the end goal, which is what you want to be intentional about, but it's not enough. You also need to understand what others want. This is why almost all intentional design processes begin with empathy or understanding the needs and experiences of your core users.

INTENTIONAL DESIGN STARTS WITH EMPATHY

Empathy involves observing and understanding what people face in their day-to-day experience, and surfacing the drivers and motivators of their behaviors. To do this, you need to understand people's environment and how they interact with their environment. You have to know what you want—and then get a sense of what they want. It's not just about their choices and actions. It's about their why, and getting a sense of their experiences and motivations. Understanding the core needs of your target community is helpful for them and you. It ultimately helps you see where God's direction, your gifts and experiences, and their needs intersect.

The practice of empathy gives you wider insight into how and why people act. It's more than just listening to them; it's seeing them in their environment and perceiving what they aren't even aware that they are doing. When people act without thinking it through first, they show you how they unconsciously interact with the world around them. When you pay attention to how people enter and leave a building, who they talk to (and don't talk to) in leaving church, where they sit in a coffee shop, or where they like to leave their keys, it indicates how an "imperfectly tailored environment" provokes a response in them that they are not even aware of.[2] Recognizing these unconscious acts gives you opportunities for unique insights and can drive unique new solutions.

If you're a leader who cares about those leaving your organization, you can seek to understand what these individual's life experiences are like so you can understand why they're making specific choices. If you're a pastor of a local church, you can try to understand why people come to your services . . . and why people don't. We can all consider the experiences of our teams—as well as that of your clientele or audience. Why do they care about the mission? What makes them feel cared for and included? What are their stresses and concerns? No matter what leadership role you fill, these questions can help you grow in empathy.

ARCHITECTING YOUR FUTURE

Clarity and empathy empower you for action. Once you understand what you want and empathize with the people who you depend on to take that action, you can respond intentionally through great design to develop a solution that helps you realize your vision for a better future.

To do this, you need to be creative and approach it like an architect of the future and use design principles. The word *architect* comes from a Greek root meaning *builder*. The forces of place and technology don't have to drive you; you can use design to drive them. The clarity and empathy you bring to the act of building make your work effective and sustainable.

Many wise people have thought long and hard about intentional design. There are many processes taught in university settings that provide various methods for designing solutions to complex problems. We'll share the three common and effective approaches that many organizations use today: human-centered design, Agile development methodology, and Lean Startup. You can immediately apply each of these three approaches to any problem you're trying to solve.

Human-Centered Design

Human-centered design is a creative approach that focuses (as you might think) on the human. IDEO's Design Toolkit describes it as "a process that starts with the people you're designing for and ends with new solutions that are tailor made to suit their needs."[3] It's about developing empathy with those for whom you're designing. It means understanding their experiences and then generating ideas and building numerous prototypes. After this, you share what you've made with them, and eventually release your inventive solution into the world.[4]

These principles are helpful if you want to understand better the experience of the people you serve. They remind you not to think about design as being about *us vs. them* or *us for them*. Human-centered design is incarnational in its very nature because it invites you to be *us with them* and as one of them.

Agile Development Methodology

Agile development methodology builds on the principles of human-centered design with a focus on rapid iteration. Initially designed for use in software development, the process emphasizes "incremental delivery, team collaboration, continual planning, and continual learning instead of trying to deliver it all at once near the end."[5] Agile focuses on creating an effective, simple process that develops minimum viable products (MVPs). These products go through multiple repeated development cycles, with regular feedback and improvement, before they are finalized. The method is a forceful, focused process that harnesses all team members to work on the same objectives.[6]

These principles help you with the continuous improvement of your processes, products, and practices. They invite you to keep growing and improving. In our nature as humans, each of us keeps learning and applying new things, and Agile methodology teaches us to enjoy the process.

Lean Startup

The third set of design principles comes from *The Lean Startup*. It provides a process-oriented approach to creating and managing new initiatives (often startups) and getting products into users' hands more quickly. It's a principled approach to product development that, as entrepreneur and author Eric Ries explains, basically teaches you how to drive an initiative—how to steer, when to accelerate, and when to turn.[7] Lean Startup was created to reconnect the products to the users more closely and more effectively, validating that they actually met their needs and were what they wanted.

These principles help you ensure that your processes, products, and practices meet your people's actual needs. Lean Startup was developed to counteract the gut instinct that drove so many startups to think they had the magic formula or product but lacked a way to understand it early in the process.

THERE IS A BETTER WAY

You may be relying on the way you've always done things because it's comfortable, familiar, or easy—but you don't have to because there's a *better* way to approach how you design solutions. You can use tried and true design processes, such as the ones we just looked at, to help you intentionally explore other possibilities to fulfill your vision. These processes will help push you to think differently and see new possibilities.

None of them are in themselves the singular answer, but together they represent a different vision. Albert Einstein has famously been attributed with saying, "We can't solve problems by using the same kind of thinking we used when we created them."[8] The tried and true approaches allow you to modify your thinking so you can arrive at a different result. The three methodologies we shared with you are just a few of the many methods for designing solutions, but they illustrate the value of empathy, the importance of quick iteration, and the focus on feedback. If you aren't sure where to start, we suggest trying one of these methods.

Digital missions is a passion of ours. We worked with Aaron, the entrepreneur we mentioned in chapter 8, to help him use human-centered principles to develop a solution for unchurched nones to connect in community. Before our work with him, few leaders were actively reaching out digitally to this demographic. Even though Aaron hadn't visited all of the nations or walked in the shoes of all of the people he wanted to reach, the design process allowed him to actively collaborate with them and better understand their experience and see the world through their eyes.

How can you get started with design? Begin by asking yourself these questions:

1. What is the real need for the solution I'm envisioning? Does what we're building target that need?

2. In what environment will this solution be used? Do I really understand that environment?

3. What is the journey like for a person using this solution? How and why did they arrive at using the solution?

4. Have we built and designed the solution in a way that it's reasonably easy for someone to learn how to use it?

5. Does the solution effectively and efficiently help users accomplish the tasks for which they're using it?

Do you remember Tim, the pastor we talked about who struggled with the idea of online small groups? He wanted to convene his people differently but wasn't sure a digital space could facilitate authentic community experiences. Well, he used the Agile methodology to design a solution. This approach allowed him to try new things incrementally, continue to develop the plan as the groups grew, and inform the solution through data and feedback. The more Tim talked with the single parents, traveling professionals, and countless others who had a desire to participate virtually—and the more he connected with others through his own experience in virtual small groups—the more he saw how meeting digitally opened up a new way to gather as the local church. This form of gathering could survive work travel, sickness, local natural disaster, and was a perfect fit when his church later faced the pandemic that forced us all to meet digitally.

How can you too use Agile development? Here are some questions to start with for this design method:

1. What's your solution and who will benefit from it?

2. What's the minimum viable product that you can initially test with a group of trusted users?

3. What constraints, challenges, and opportunities exist in the development, design, and usage of your product or service?

4. Could your team have a short daily stand-up meeting to address priorities and storyboard your process?

5. What are your near-term goals? Is the product or solution you are designing helping you achieve those goals?

Lauren, the executive we worked with who feared losing control if those she led worked remotely, ended up using Lean Startup to design a solution to provide flexibility and work-life balance. She had a sense of what she wanted, and this design process gave her a pathway to develop it as quickly as possible with as little overhead as needed in close coordination with her team. The lean approach allowed Lauren to assess the cultural norms preventing them from gathering in places other than their corporate headquarters. As she did, she realized that distributing her workforce provided more opportunities to connect directly with the customers, which improved their ability to deliver the product or service they offered. Lauren also recognized that the validated learning Lean Startup provided allowed her to let employees grow in different ways, and helped shift the focus off of the product and onto what they could learn and prove together.

The five principles of Lean Startup methodology are:

1. Entrepreneurs are everywhere—in every sphere and sector of life.

2. Entrepreneurship is management. It's more than a product; it's also a process to manage.

3. Validated learning is as valuable as, if not more than, creating products—it proves hypotheses and builds business.

4. Innovation accounting matters to improve outcomes, measure progress, and prioritize work.

5. There's a build-measure-learn loop that focuses on feedback and gives you the insight you need to know to succeed.[9]

Design helped each of these leaders to see a future that they were otherwise unable to see. They started with the clarity of what they wanted and then landed on an approach to help them get there.

RESPONDING TO WHAT YOU WANT INSTEAD OF REACTING TO WHAT YOU FEAR

Ten or twenty years from now, you're unlikely to regret the things you did as much as the things you didn't do—the things you didn't try, the frontiers you didn't explore, the risks you didn't take. Yet there's so much inertia and many genuine barriers that keep us from acting.

If you're still reading this book, it's because you aren't satisfied with the status quo. You aren't interested in settling for the current design or staying on the present trajectory. You believe there's a better future ahead and want to respond out of a better understanding of what your users want. Design offers you the power to create change and add value to the lives of others. When something looks beautiful and works well, when it does what it's supposed to do, it sparks an emotional connection. People want to use it or be part of it and it changes the way they experience life.

By rethinking his design approach and understanding the core needs of the user, Aaron designed a better approach to reaching the unchurched nones through digital missions, Tim developed a solution that met the needs of the congregants in his local church, and Lauren embraced a more agile approach that better engaged teams across her organization. How will you approach the design process differently than you currently do?

Based on the work you have already done in the previous chapters to identify in Christ, connect with others, belong in community, and gather virtually, which approach would be best for you? Pick an approach you're going to try and write it down on your Future Canvas worksheet. You can always change later if it doesn't seem to fit. We'll continue to build on it in the next three chapters.

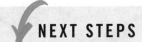

NEXT STEPS

1. When you gather with your community, what do you work on together? What are you trying to design?

2. What kind of thinking got you to the problem you have (remember the Einstein quote)? Is there a better way to respond than you have historically taken?

3. Which design methodology resonates most with you? Which doesn't? Why?

4. Are there other approaches to design that you can think of which might work better for you?

5. What can you do today to get started on designing a better solution to help you realize a better future?

COLLABORATE

Alone we can do so little; together we can do so much.[1]

—HELEN KELLER

We identify in Christ (chapter 5), relate to others (chapter 6), and belong in community (chapter 7) so that we can gather together (chapter 8), design better solutions (chapter 9), and **collaborate** with others (chapter 10). At the intersection of place, technology, and purpose, we explore how to actively engage with others to work toward our shared, preferred future.

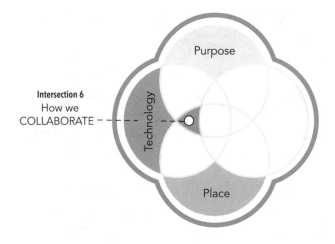

As the battlefields of World War II stretched thousands of miles around the globe—from Rome, Berlin, and Tokyo to Madagascar and the Aleutian Islands—the conventional land-based approaches to war no longer worked. This new worldwide conflict wasn't characterized by monumental battles, glorious victories, or conquered landscapes, which had been common throughout history. Now it was vital to control both the air and the sea, which meant the Allied countries needed a new approach.

During this time, aircraft carriers became the most critical ships in the navy. They were able to launch air attacks from anywhere in the ocean. With a combat area that spanned virtually every part of the world, aircraft carriers could easily navigate the water and safely deliver a concerted attack within a few hundred miles of any target.

This type of war became "a test of nerves and ingenuity." Both sides had to develop tools and methods of fighting previously unimaginable. It called for unprecedented creativity, perseverance, and endurance.[2] Each day, naval aviators launched from aircraft carriers to pursue their mission, and each night they returned to the same aircraft carrier located in the middle of a dark and vast ocean. Many of the planes were damaged and in need of repair.

A primary advantage of an aircraft carrier—its ability to relocate to any navigable part of the world—was also a key disadvantage. Access to spare parts was limited at best. With no factories nearby, parts had to be salvaged off of other damaged aircraft and planes rebuilt overnight. Using limited parts and supplies, the mechanics would pull all-nighters to "hack" together a solution. They rebuilt airframes, repaired engines, and recovered guns. Our friend Charlie shared this powerful story he heard firsthand from his father, Art Auvermann:

> He is 92, active, and a veteran of WWII. He pointed out that he first heard the term "hacker" during the early days of WWII in the South Pacific. The U.S. Navy was not prepared for war and was getting beaten pretty badly. He was

there. When fighter planes would return from action, they would be shot up and, in many cases, crashed on landing because their pilots were injured. Each night huge teams of mechanics would converge upon the wrecked planes and "hack" at them, removing the good parts from each to build a new plane overnight out of all the salvaged pieces. He told me they were referred to as the "hacker details." That was because they had to use metal "hacksaws" as they cut away the damaged panels of the planes. At 92, he seems to think that is the original root of the term because he said it was very commonly used during the war 60 years ago.[3]

While we don't know exactly how many planes were damaged in World War II and repaired during these all-night hackathons, we do know the success of D-Day and the Normandy campaign likely wouldn't have been possible without the ingenuity and collaborative spirit of these unspoken heroes. Because their cause mattered greatly, they used what they had to make in unconventional ways what they needed.

COLLABORATION VERSUS COMPETITION

It wasn't only the advent of the sea and air technologies that changed the way battles were fought during World War II. In the opening line of his book, *How the War Was Won*, author Phillips Payson O'Brien observes that "there were no decisive battles in World War II."[4] Combat in the conventional sense didn't win the war. Instead, victory resulted from an active collaboration by more than thirty countries that worked together. These countries, known as the Allied forces, recognized that they needed to collaborate, not compete, to fend off Germany and Japan, who had joined together with a common purpose.

The Allied forces understood that war was no longer happening in just one localized place, but that it now extended to nearly every corner of the world. They knew that technology was advancing rapidly and that lethal weapons could be delivered from a great distance by a missile. No country—no matter how big its economy, how large its capacity to produce weaponry, or how many people it could deploy—could respond effectively alone.

World War II was fought over years and involved each of the Allied forces' economic abilities and capacity to produce and deploy weaponry to respond to the growing global threat. What ultimately sealed the fate for the German and Japanese defeat was the destruction of their aircraft, warships, and submarines. This new type of globalized war could never have been won without the collaboration of the Allied countries.

PURPOSE + TECHNOLOGY + PLACE

We often define collaboration as "people working together," but it's much more than that. The Futures Framework places collaboration between design and scale because collaboration's a critical link between your process for solving problems and your approach to grow and scale those solutions.

As we addressed in the last chapter, design starts with clarity about your purpose and what you want. It continues with how you use technology to solve that problem more effectively. Next, it adds place to identify new places to serve, connect, and contribute.

Place is also a specific driver in how we collaborate. Serving in World War II is very different from working in a specialized government agency. Living in a small town in the Midwest is very different from life in a big city. Collaboration takes that particular place or context and uses technology—from simple to complex—to find a better solution to a shared problem or to help support a shared purpose. It's the collaborative work itself that turns design into scale.

Does that mean we don't need people for collaboration? Absolutely not! People drive collaboration, and all of their diversity simply makes that collaboration richer. But it's the variation in purpose, place, and technology that has the most significant impact on how we engage in working toward our shared future.

WHAT COLLABORATION IS NOT

Collaboration's a buzzword that's thrown around a lot these days. The last time we searched online, we received 3,340,000,000 results in just 0.62 seconds. (Thanks, Google—your technology is impressive!) Nearly every major publication on business and innovation has issued a story about the importance of collaboration, but there's still some unfortunate confusion about what collaboration is exactly.

In a conversation with one of our clients, we discussed an article citing a decision by an IBM executive to bring employees back to the office.[5] Her decision was easy to understand: she wanted IBM to become the best place to work and, for her to do this, she wanted to create a collaborative environment.

As we discussed in chapter 8, the belief that it's easier to work together when we have authentic relationships and that it's easier to build those relationships when we work face-to-face and side by side isn't unfounded. According to leadership expert and author Jesse Lyn Stoner, "Coordination and cooperation is essential for effective and efficient work . . . research supports the notion that some face-to-face time makes a big difference." The mistake many make is to assume that this is collaboration when it's simply coordination and cooperation. But what's the difference between the three? "*Coordination* is sharing information and resources so that each party can accomplish their part in support of a mutual objective. It is about teamwork in implementation. Not creating something new."[6] Similarly, cooperation is when individuals support each others' goals by exchanging relevant information and resources. Stoner notes that because cooperation lacks a shared goal, there's no shared purpose. "Something new may be achieved as a result," she explains, "but it arises from the individual, not from a collective team effort."[7]

Collaboration, on the other hand, is what Stoner defines as "working together to create something new in support of a shared vision."[8] The key point is that collaboration isn't an individual effort. It's a shared effort that's united around a common purpose. What results is the creation of something new that couldn't have been generated individually.

We may dream about accomplishing individual work, skeptical that collaborating with others is the best way to achieve our needs. But when we jump in and serve others' work, our hearts, visions, and gifts come alive. Plus, as Christians, we're called to collaboration. In 1 Corinthians 3:9, the apostle Paul writes that we're co-laborers or fellow workers with God in His work. Co-laborers are more than friends or helpers. The word denotes those who work side by side to share the heavy lifting for a purpose bigger than their own. It's when we co-labor that we begin to see our work with a new vision.

BUILDING A BETTER GOVERNMENT

A few years ago, we had a chance to see the benefits of collaboration up close. We were working with several federal agencies that kept getting stuck. They were stuck with the narrowness of their mandate, the limitations of resources, the restrictions of regulations, and the slowness of their decision-making processes. These agencies were so constrained that they couldn't find a path forward. All their energy was focused on the near-term objective that it felt impossible for them to expand their vision or scope, regardless of how much they wanted to do so. Don't we all know what that feels like?

To help them get unstuck, we had to reframe the challenge that was holding them back. In pursuit of each of their missions, they'd missed one of the most important aspects of government. The answer for these organizations was hidden in the very nature of government as a "mechanism for *collective* action." Citizens come together in order to make laws and policies to promote their common welfare. They develop the institutions of government to manage problems that are too big for them to handle as individuals and whose solutions are in the common interest.[9]

Together, we wondered what would be possible if we looked at their problems through the lens of collaboration. We didn't have to look far for inspiration. Thomas Jefferson talked about this type of government in a letter he wrote in 1816. It's a government where "every man . . . feels that he is a participator in the government of affairs, not merely at an election one day in the year, but every day."[10] The government Jefferson envisioned was a collaboration where every citizen worked together for the common benefit of the nation. He talked about how our government was always supposed to be collaborative, but somewhere along the lines of history, government became something else—something closed and far from participatory.

Governments around the world often get a bad rap for being outdated, opaque, inefficient, and even corrupt—and many are. We've seen it firsthand. Understandably, this has led people globally to demand a new approach. There's a call for more civic participation in public affairs, which includes discovering ways to make governments more responsive and effective.[11]

THE NATIONAL DAY OF CIVIC HACKING

Traditionally, the government agencies have been focused on one *purpose* (like building roads in a state or combating drug trafficking in a nation), one *place* (a local city, for example), or one set of *technologies* (such as weather satellites, traffic cameras, or jet airplanes). It's rare for agencies to cross lines and learn from each other's data or experience. Similarly, citizen needs seldom get addressed from across the levels, where the state attends to what's happening at the city level, and the states then pass lessons up to the federal level.

But what if a local city library could share its resources with others, such as making its data available to state universities? What if a city could share its lessons on managing homeless shelters with federal government agencies charged with solving the same problem? What happens when our government learns from itself and benefits from the work and the learning at every level?

If anyone should collaborate, it should be our government entities. Admittedly, doing this is hard for the government. Although it's a platform for collective action, it's not an efficient one at connecting people in many cases.

To evolve our government in the digital age—when old approaches have been disrupted by the forces of place, purpose, and technology—we set out to form a new collaboration. In 2013, we invited friends in different agencies to join us as we started the National Day of Civic Hacking. It's one of the largest peacetime collaboration efforts to apply the collective genius of citizens to the problems they collectively face at the city, state, and national levels.

Since then, the National Day of Civic Hacking has become an annual gathering that brings together developers, analysts, project managers, and concerned citizens to collaboratively develop new solutions using publicly released data to improve governance. Civic hacking refers to a creative and often technological approach to solving civic problems. It's working together overnight to hack together solutions that add value to the lives of citizens. The idea is simply a modern version of hacking together planes on an aircraft carrier deep in a dark ocean so that we can accomplish our mission.

Our goal was to do everything we could to connect people, not only to develop new technology or solve tough problems but to fundamentally help government retrace its roots. To make it more participatory. And the National Day of Civic Hacking has done just that. It's created a place—one weekend every year—for citizens to come together and do their part to improve life for everyone. The relationships built, the insight gained, the data shared, and the projects developed have all carried far beyond the weekend. These things have changed the way agencies address challenges every day of the year.

Tens of thousands of citizens in over 100 cities across the United

States come together to work on problems as small as fixing potholes and as large as helping launch rockets into space. By joining with others from across the nation, using technology, and working together on common challenges, we're able to improve the cities we live in and the governments that serve them.

Today, making a difference in government is no longer limited to showing up to vote on election day, sending a letter to your representative, expressing your concern by protesting, or accepting a government job. The best government for the people is government by the people. Through collaborations like the National Day of Civic Hacking, you too can now work with others who fundamentally care about government and want to contribute to the future of our world.[12] Through collaboration, we've increased the chance that our government lives up to its true potential—of the people, by the people, and for the people.

WHY WE DON'T COLLABORATE

Sounds amazing, right? So why don't these things happen more often? Collaboration doesn't come easily to most of us. It's added work, at least initially, and can take more time than other approaches. At the mention of collaboration, one of our clients protested wildly, "That's too many cooks in the kitchen!" We responded if we wanted to cook for more than just ourselves, we had to get more chefs involved. Besides the added work and time, there are several other good reasons we don't collaborate.

Sometimes we can't get past the urgent. Leadership can be overwhelming at times. It's tempting to stick with familiar approaches or count our losses and think small rather than count the possibilities and think big.

Sometimes we don't value the contributions of those who are different than us because we fear those differences. As a result, we narrow our purpose and focus. We stick to what we know and make an enemy of what we don't know. It's easier to fear those who are different than to recognize the gifts of their diversity.

Sometimes we too narrowly define our place. We naturally think about ourselves without understanding the broader context. We believe our world is *the* world, and we forget that others share the same challenges we do. Humans naturally trust what they see, so proximity carries a lot of weight in what we value and who we trust.

Sometimes we avoid technology. It's different and unfamiliar. Or we over-trust the technology, hoping it holds the answer to all our problems. When, instead, the technology is just a mechanism to work and connect differently.

Sometimes—and far too often—we don't collaborate because it feels like a personal failure of our leadership. "Needing" the ideas and contributions of others feels like inadequacy.

All of these realities separate and isolate us, making it impossible to collaborate. We might be able to share information and resources with others, but we're unable to unite around a common purpose and create something new that couldn't have been generated individually. Collaboration challenges us to realize that if we genuinely want to achieve our preferred future, we need to work with others to do so. We aren't the one person with the one insight that makes all the difference.

THE ESSENCE OF COLLABORATION

We work with a lot of leaders who desire to collaborate but don't know where to start. We explain it like this: there are essentials and nonessentials. Don't compromise on what's essential, but be willing to partner with others on the nonessentials.

What are the things that are absolutely necessary, extremely important, and essential to your preferred future? If you're a pastor of a local church, you'd say your essential beliefs—the core, uncompromisable tenets of your faith, such as the resurrection of Christ. As a leader, you have essentials that are never changing and foundational to who you are. They drive the very mission of your organization, church, or ministry. These essentials are important because they help you navigate your complex and changing world. They are critical for your survival. But everything isn't—and can't be—essential. This is the most significant mistake most leaders we work with make. Without clarity on this point, it's easy to make everything essential. When you do this, though, you unconsciously limit what's possible. This constrains who you're willing to work with and the approaches you're willing to try out.

It's possible to collaborate with others similar to you who share your essentials, but it's much more likely to find leaders who are very different from you, but who are willing to collaborate with you on the nonessentials. If you can identify these organizations, churches, and ministries that bring a diversity of thought to the table *and* share the same essential priorities, the magic will happen. But be careful not to define your team so narrowly that you miss out on the innovation that comes when you invite a far wider community of people into the conversation.

ESSENTIALS AND NONESSENTIALS

Collaboration starts by identifying what's essential and what's not. What would it look like for you to collaborate with others? What would you work on, and with whom would you collaborate? What is truly essential and not essential?

Based on the work you've already done in the previous chapters to identify in Christ, connect with others, belong in community, gather, and design an approach, who will you collaborate with? We've noted some constraints that might hold you back and showed you how to identify your core essentials so you can invite new partners into the process.

At this point, consider who you need to invite into collaboration with you to help solve the problem you share in common. Take some time to brainstorm who might share your vision and contribute something that's currently lacking that you are unable to provide. How might others see it differently? Try to think beyond the first idea that naturally pops into your head. In reality, there might be great potential in collaborating with a different type of church, a secular organization, or city government. You can jot all of this down on your Future Canvas worksheet.

NEXT STEPS

1. What are the constraints that keep you isolated and from collaborating actively with others? Where does it feel easier just to do it yourself?

2. Do you sometimes settle for cooperation or coordination? What would it take for you to actually co-labor with others?

3. What is essential to you? What is nonessential for you? Why?

4. What makes an ideal collaborator for you and your organization? What are the essentials that need to be the same to allow a productive collaboration?

5. What's the most significant barrier or constraint to collaboration for your team right now?

11

SCALE

Aim at Heaven and you will get Earth "thrown in":
aim at Earth and you get neither.[1]

—C. S. LEWIS

We identify in Christ (chapter 5), relate to others (chapter 6), and belong in community (chapter 7) so that we can gather together (chapter 8) to design solutions (chapter 9) and collaborate with others (chapter 10) to **scale** our vision (chapter 11). At the intersection of technology and purpose, we explore how to scale our vision.

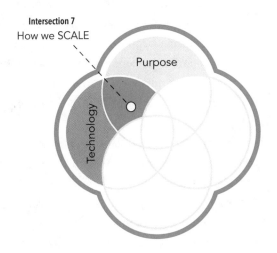

MATH IS FUN—REALLY

Do you remember when you asked your high school algebra teacher, "How is this actually going to help me in the real world?" Well, today is that day. To better understand how scale works, you first need to appreciate the difference between scale and growth. Scale isn't the same as growth. Growth is about becoming larger over time, while scale is about escalation. One is linear; the other is exponential.

Let's consider it by revisiting a story you may have heard during that algebra class. There was once a father who grumbled that his son's five-dollar a week allowance was too high. His son responded, "Okay, Dad. How about this? You give me a penny for the first day of the month, two cents for the second, four cents for the next, eight cents for the next, and so on for every day of the month."[2] The father gladly agreed.

Was the father or the son more clever? You're right—the son! This is about exponential growth. By doubling every day, the son's allowance grew from one penny on the first day to a total of $10,737,418.24 at the end of the month!

Using algebra, you learned that doubling a small number over and over soon compounds to large numbers. This concept applies as much to financial investments as it does to the replication of bacteria. It's the phenomenon that's the active force behind scale. This basic principle is core to many significant economic developments, such as the Industrial Revolution. And it's why bigger companies are often more efficient and can deliver goods and services at a lower price than their competition while still making a profit.

Scaling is the goal of most church-planting movements around the world. They aren't hoping to merely sustain the total number of churches they've planted or incrementally grow by adding a few churches every year or so. Instead, they're focused on the compound or multiplying effect of two churches becoming four, and four churches becoming eight to ten, and so forth. The premise is that actual multiplicative growth is only possible when new churches are being started by the churches themselves—rather than solely by professional church planters or missionaries.

DON'T DESPISE SMALL BEGINNINGS

It's not only true about churches, though. A similar story is proverbially told about the inventor of chess. In return for his achievement, he asked the king for one kernel of wheat for the first square on the board, two for the second, four for the third, and so on. The king agreed readily, and the inventor smiled. Courtiers continued to bring in the portions of wheat until they realized that the inventor had laid claim to more grain than was in the royal storehouse.

It's easy to feel small when we're at two kernels or four kernels or thirty-six kernels. When we're at one hundred users for our app, or two hundred people in our congregation, growth in the way we want to see it seems infinitely far away. But futurist Ray Kurzweil calls the point of exponential growth "the second half of the chessboard."[3] Initially, the curve of the exponential trend—the first half of the chessboard—is so flat that it doesn't look like a trend. We get stuck with a linear perspective. This is where a lot of us are: Still in the first half and still growing a little at a time. Working hard for the small wins and feeling like we might as well give up. But if we can press forward and trust in what God has in store, the future will be very different than we can imagine today.

Your vision doesn't have to grow into the billions . . . but what if it could? Either way, it *should* grow into its full potential. This is what scale is about: seeing every person, project, and program meet the needs of everyone it can, with all of us growing in the process.

HOW TO START A MOVEMENT

Movements are broadly defined as anything where organized groups purposefully work together towards a common goal. Scaling is a primary driver for their success. Movements become successful when they don't just grow incrementally, but scale exponentially. There are many types of movements—civil rights movements, church planting movements, social change movements—and no clear-cut recipe to follow. One of the primary ingredients to scaling a movement, though, is inviting others to participate. When TED wanted to expand the scale of their organization, they created TEDx, which empowered organizers from around the world to plan local events. When Google wanted to engage their developer community, they invited developers around the world to host local events, and they now have 600 chapters globally.[4]

In the Futures Framework, scale is located at the intersection of the forces of purpose and technology. It's easy to see how technology can help people fulfill their purpose. It helped TEDx go multisite while maintaining its core culture and vision, and it helped Google invite people into carrying out its core mission. But purpose helps keep technology on track as well, making it useful and focused. Marshall McLuhan famously reminded people that "the medium is the message."[5] So often the channel we hear through (whether radio, television, web, or something entirely different) becomes the one medium we pay attention to, and we lose sight of the communication itself. But a real vision opened up with effectual technology is what makes scaling possible.

When we wanted to scale our vision for NASA, we started a movement. At the time, NASA had a clear purpose of improving life on Earth and in space, and we wanted to increase our limited capacity to realize that grand vision. Our problem was that we knew it would require many more people than the 20,000 scientists and engineers that were directly paid by NASA. We knew we needed to invite others outside of NASA to contribute directly and tangibly to space exploration. So we invited organizers from around the world to host a local event to help us develop new products and new approaches to exploration. Via technology, we connected a global community of over 25,000 citizens from more than 100 countries around the world. In just one weekend, over 1,000 new solutions were developed to the challenges we'd invited them to respond to. Nearly a decade later, the International Space Apps Challenge is still going strong, and NASA continues to engage a diverse volunteer community from all corners of the world, all age ranges, and all skill types, to collaborate to accomplish its mission.

All of these shifts were about creating ownership. More people needed to pitch—and hear—ideas worth spreading than TED could fit in one conference center in Vancouver every year. Google could only directly touch so many people themselves as they organize the world's information. Space exploration had to be a vision carried by more than just the engineers and scientists at NASA. For something to go from a good idea to an actual movement, more people have to take ownership of it and see themselves in it. Our passion at NASA wasn't about building the best rocket, solving medical mysteries in a science lab, or walking on the farthest planet, although those things all sounded awesome. It was about engaging the unique skills and passions of every human being on Earth into the human exploration of the universe.

IT'S NOT ABOUT YOU (OR ABOUT ME)

"It's not about you," is the opening declaration in the popular book, *The Purpose-Driven Life*.[6] This bestselling book has deeply impacted many leaders since its release. Christian or not, people have flocked to a book they hoped would help them find their purpose in life.

If you've read it, you know that when you dig into the book, you discover how true that opening statement is. It's not about you. It's about others. As Christians, we know this because of what happened at the end of Jesus' life. Just before the resurrected Christ ascended, after spending forty days on Earth, He gave His disciples one final command: "Go therefore and make disciples of all nations, baptizing them in the name of the Father and of the Son and of the Holy Spirit, teaching them to observe all that I have commanded you. And behold, I am with you always, to the end of the age." The full text of this command, known as the Great Commission, is recorded in Matthew 28:18–20 and is also found in the other three gospels.

There's no task we're commissioned to as Christians like the Great Commission. It's the central purpose of the Christian church, and accordingly, of every Christian. This purpose drives everything we do, and it's much bigger than ourselves. It isn't just a command for evangelists or missionaries; it's for *everyone*. Believers are called to share the good news about Jesus to every tongue, tribe, and nation—and not just to tell them about it, but teach them to obey it. Obedience is the measure of success. People know that we follow Him because we obey His commands. And the Great Commission isn't finished yet. There are still nations and people who haven't heard, so we still need to go and tell them.

It's a huge task. Jesus' command to reach all nations has motivated pastors and missionaries all over the world. But not one of them thinks they can accomplish the Great Commission on their own.

HACK4MISSIONS: TECHNOLOGY AND PURPOSE

Technology has given Christians new ways to connect, gather in both physical and digital spaces, collaborate, and design new approaches. Many actively employ technology to securely and safely communicate, coordinate gatherings, and worship together. But, as a digital missionary, our good friend Mark W. Breneman writes, "As missional Christians, we need to stop thinking of technology merely as a tool, like a shovel, and start thinking of technology as both a tool to reach people *and the mission field itself!*"[7]

What it means to be on mission, serve others, and be a global church is being redefined right in front of us—and it's what happens at the intersection of purpose and technology that's making this a reality. Creative solutions based on technological advancements and fueled by a common purpose have the potential to allow the church to scale in ways it's never been able to before. As this happens, the growth curve of technology won't be linear; it'll be exponential.[8] The pace of change will only grow faster over time. As we write this, there are now nearly as many connected devices as there are people in the world.[9] Some remote villages even have smartphones before running water. Billions of people "have access to the gospel in the palm of their hands."[10]

We've been fortunate to have a front seat as Christians embrace their purpose and use technology to scale their vision to reach the unreached population groups. We've organized hundreds of innovation events, such as Hack4Missions, to convene inventors, developers, and technologists who have a passion for using technology in the mission field. Technologies like machine learning, artificial intelligence, and software automation hold great promise for missionaries working in persecuted and oppressed countries. At one event recently, we worked with an organization to use steganography—"the practice of concealing a file, message, image, or video within another file, message, image, or video"[11]—to develop an app that allows Christians to communicate with one another securely. Technology allows us to close security gaps in communication that governments can exploit to identify Christians. It can be used to evade security protocols and defend against hostile regimes.

THE GROWTH TRAP

When we talk about scale, a mistake you may be tempted to make as a leader is to focus on the wrong thing. In our culture, the drive for exponential growth can cause more problems than it solves. For example, our focus shouldn't be on how many people gather or the number of conversions. Rather, we need to focus on the impact we hope to have and the people's lives we hope to change.

Bigger isn't always better, but it's easy to think it is. We live in Texas, where everything's bigger, and in American culture, we equate bigger with stronger, smarter, and more effective. But the problem is that bigger often turns people into a number. As author and blogger Jeremy Meyers explains, "Almost anyone can gather 10,000 people. But loving those the world hates, helping rescue someone from addiction, or showing people that they're loved by God is a spiritual victory which cannot be replicated, duplicated, systematized, or multiplied."[12] Your preferred vision for the future isn't about gathering 10,000 people; it's about impacting your world. Scaling your vision is about meeting needs—whether through your community, your products, or your small groups.

SO WHERE'S YOUR MOVEMENT?

Some clients we've worked with believed the secret was simply in having a strong vision—after all, who can deny a leader with vision, right? Or, they thought it was in incredible planning of the metrics and the processes. While those things are great, they won't scale your preferred future. Here's what will.

Tell the Story

Once you've designed your solution and engaged with others to collaborate on it, you have to be able to explain it to people. Communicate your why—and why it's different from the status quo. Tell the story of why it matters. When we started doing this for the International Space Apps Challenge, all kinds of people were ambivalent.

Wasn't NASA canceled when the Space Shuttle retired?

Did we really go to the moon anyway?

But I'm not an astronaut.

Why would we spend money on space exploration when there are problems on Earth?

. . . and on and on. We addressed every one of these questions and concerns individually, sometimes hundreds of times. We told the stories of life in space changing life on Earth and reminded people of the value of the work in every sphere. We shared the story of the exploration still to be done and why it makes us human.

While many initiatives, companies, products, and churches take a niche approach to satisfy themselves in their circles, common causes are what change the world. Not everyone necessarily wants to be an astronaut or fly in space . . . but if we connect them to their inner explorer and remind them of the innate curiosity we all have, then they begin to see themselves in our cause of space exploration. Not everyone wants to be a missionary . . . but if we remind them of the universal need to hear the gospel and how no one can hear unless someone goes, then they begin to see themselves in our cause of missions.

Use Data and Technology to Open Doors

Technology is a means, not an end. Understanding this distinction made an incredible difference with Hack4Missions. Technology circumvented the need for people to fly to the other side of the world, or experience life themselves in the far reaches of the planet. It allowed us to see and talk to the people we wanted to serve. Sometimes it was as simple as a video call and a conversation with a missionary, or as complex as remote navigating drones onto sides of mountains in war zones. As technology becomes easier, cheaper, and quicker to connect, the world becomes smaller.

Data analytics has a huge impact too. We have an unprecedented glimpse online into who reads our content and how they respond to it. We know more about our audience and our communities than ever before—who is reading our websites, what they're clicking on, and what they're searching for. Church planters can target cities and neighborhoods with information granular to the household: political and religious affiliations, race and ethnicity, family size, types of cars they drive, and even how much they owe on their home.

Additionally, social media has given us a direct connection to all those potential listeners. Significant public figures from the pope to the president to the most popular celebrities now speak to us directly and unfiltered. Our stories no longer have to go through others to get to our community. For example, one of our friends pastors a small mainline church in a medium-size town. The church hosts about a hundred people in its building on a Sunday morning. But our friend later posts his quite entertaining sermons on YouTube, and gets double or triple the audience—and his viewers are from all around the world. So, who's "his church"? Is it just the people who live in his town and affiliate with his denomination? Or is his sphere of influence and opportunity much wider?

Focus on Engagement

Finally, scale is about engagement or the energy, enthusiasm, and focus that demonstrates commitment. The most impactful efforts invite everyone to see themselves in them and make contributions that help shape the outcome. Simply put, almost everyone wants something to do, and they want to care about it. They want a way to contribute and add value. Engagement means people do more without being asked. They go above and beyond because it's not just a job—they have ownership in it.

We're focusing on engagement when we aren't just counting those who attend, but those who follow. We're looking at those who are giving, volunteering, and showing up not because the pastor told them to, but because they feel a part of the mission. If you focus on engagement, you'll naturally get attendance in the end. You'll get customers or clients. Mission is what matters. If you have clarity on your vision, can tell the story of your why, and invite people into it, scale will start to emerge.

So, ask yourself: What's true about your work that people can see themselves in? What are you reminding them of that culture tells them to forget? What's the thing you're offering them so that your vision can become our vision? What's the thing they can do to be part of it? Because when *you* becomes *us* . . . you've built the foundation for scale.

TO THE ENDS OF THE EARTH

Let's go back to that grand scale challenge that Jesus gave us. The Great Commission is an intimidatingly large and grand vision. As we write this, there are about eight billion people on the planet, in anywhere from 15,000 to 24,000 different people groups (depending on how you define the boundaries between people groups). It's estimated that there are 218 unreached, unengaged people groups with at least 500 in population. These groups are still dwelling in their ancestral homelands and have never had the chance to hear about Jesus.[13] That's between five and six million people.

If you're just one person, in one church, with the mission to reach eight billion people, it seems impossible. Learning all those languages? Translating the Scriptures? Figuring out how to engage with cultures that are very different from yours? The challenge is much bigger than that. The Great Commission's incredible calling is one that can't happen unless the whole community gathers, shares their gifts, and designs a plan to collaborate. Fulfilling the global task and reaching the eight billion people on our planet requires all of us, over many lifetimes and many generations. It's not someone else's to do. It has to be all of ours.

Your purpose can't be accomplished alone, either. So, how can you invite others to contribute to it? What can you do to start a movement using technology to scale your vision?

Based on the work you've already done in the previous chapters to identify in Christ, connect with others, belong in community, gather virtually, design an approach, and collaborate with others, how will you scale your vision? And remember, scaling isn't about big numbers. It's about inviting others to help you realize the better, preferred future you've envisioned, as well as recognizing that more people than just you could benefit from it. At this point, crystallize how you can start small to scale your vision. Write it down on your Future Canvas worksheet.

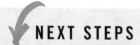

NEXT STEPS

1. Is growth a temptation for you, or a pressure from your leadership?

2. Does scaling feel overwhelming to you? Does it feel easier just to do your own thing right now?

3. How relevant does your purpose feel beyond your immediate team or community? How big could you see your vision getting? What would happen if you multiply that by ten?

4. How can technology help you amplify your mission and accomplish it?

5. What are the barriers that keep you from scaling?

IMPACT

How wonderful it is that no one has to wait,
but can start right now to gradually change the world.[1]
—ANNE FRANK

We identify in Christ (chapter 5), relate to others (chapter 6), and belong in community (chapter 7) so that we can gather together (chapter 8) to design solutions (chapter 9) and collaborate with others (chapter 10) to scale our vision (chapter 11) in order to have an **impact** (chapter 12) on the world.

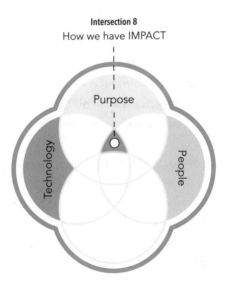

Intersection 8
How we have IMPACT

According to a Swedish study, Monday is the most common day of the week for heart attacks.[2] Researchers found that the risk of experiencing a heart attack on Monday is 11 percent higher than it is from Tuesday to Friday. And, for those working, that risk increases to 20 percent.[3] While the study cites a few factors that may influence why this day ranks as the highest, stress is a significant one.

We believe that this stress is a result of what happens when people are engaged in meaningless work. They're overwhelmed by the burden of what are too often meaningless tasks—and it's killing them. Psychologist Barry Schwartz observes, "Ninety percent of adults spend half their waking lives doing things they would rather not be doing at places they would rather not be."[4] This quote wouldn't make a very good inspirational wall poster, but it's true. Meaningless work leads to disengagement, disillusionment, discontentment, and for some, the increased stress that contributes to an early death.

So what would people rather be doing? They long to engage in work they find meaningful.

LONGING TO MAKE AN IMPACT

Over the last decade, people have shown a burgeoning curiosity in how to live meaningful, purpose-driven lives. The common thread is the idea that for work to be significant, an individual must pinpoint how their efforts make a meaningful contribution. People want jobs that are intentional, purposeful, and significant. They want to have an impact. They desire to be enabled and empowered to contribute to the greater good through their work.[5]

Study after study about emerging generations in the workforce point out the need to leave an impact through meaningful work in very tangible ways. One study found that 75 percent of those surveyed said they'd rather take a pay cut than work for a company that wasn't focused on having an impact.[6] They wanted more than a job or even a career. They wanted the opportunity to make a difference. They were looking for work that they would do even if they didn't get paid for it. They wanted to pursue work that truly utilized their unique gifts and talents; work that they were meant to do. But don't we all want our work to be meaningful—regardless of how long we've been in the workforce?

As a Christian leader, you're most likely familiar with the concept of impact, but it isn't just a Christian principle. Almost everyone wants their short existence to matter. They want to leave a legacy and to have their lives count for something more than simply "ashes to ashes, dust to dust."[7] This is why psychologists directly link having meaningful work to greater well-being and personal fulfillment. One review noted that "finding meaning in one's work has been shown to increase motivation, engagement, empowerment, career development, job satisfaction, individual performance and personal fulfillment."[8] Discovering meaning isn't related only to work, though. It's also part of volunteering, family life, and mentoring. Vision clarity and mission clarity bring a richness and color to every part of our human existence.

Meaning in work is also the fabric of leadership. In an article in the *Harvard Business Review*, Nick Craig and Scott A. Snook note that academics argue a leader's "most important role is to be a steward of the organization's purpose."[9] So, as a leader, whether you lead five people or 5,000, how you communicate and live out your purpose matters.

But, as Craig and Snook explain, one of the biggest obstacles to finding meaningful and impactful work is that few leaders can identify and articulate their own sense of purpose. Even fewer leaders are able to directly link their purpose to the mission statement of the organization they're leading. They may be able to articulate the organization's mission clearly, but when asked to describe how they're having an impact on this mission, they're often unable to provide a satisfying answer. "As a result," Craig and Snook write, "they limit their aspirations and often fail to achieve their most ambitious professional and personal goals."[10] If you struggle in this area, our goal in this book is to change that for you. We want to help you define and work toward your preferred future so that you can impact the world.

MORE THAN JUST A JOB

The reason for creating preferred futures isn't to be academic or to provide more options for your organization, church, or ministry. Instead, you develop preferred futures to pursue your particular vision for impact with intention. Impact is how God works through you to oversee and lead His creation and steward His gifts.

It's also the last of the lenses in the Futures Framework. Impact occurs at the intersection of purpose, people, and technology. Without it, the other seven lenses you've looked through don't have a focal point. Impact is the outcome of the compounding effect of all of these lenses combined. It's your end goal, and it's focused by purpose and amplified by technology for the sake of people.

Focused by Purpose

One of the gifts of your Christian life is your God-given purpose of following Jesus and becoming more like Him. You're called to be a disciple—a student or imitator—of *His* purposes. Being a disciple of Christ is more than a job or even a career; it's a vocation. The term *vocation* comes from the Latin word *vocare,* which means "to call."[11] As a follower of Jesus, your calling starts at the core of your identity in Christ. It then continues through the rest of the Futures Framework, which includes your relationships with others, the communities you belong to and gather with, the ways you collaborate with others, the solutions you design, and the scale you use to achieve your preferred vision.

Within this vocation, you also have your specific purpose. God created you with unique gifts, talents, and passions. When you've found your specific calling, you know it because your life is full of joy, satisfaction, and fulfillment. The Barna Group's Bill Denzel and David Kinnaman say that "work is one of the primary places we discover and define ourselves, relate to others and live out our faith day by day."[12] It's because of this we often think of our specific vocation or calling in terms of our work. However, as one church's initiative points out, your vocation isn't only what you do with your time, such as your professional work or your investment in your family. It's also who you're called to be and how you're called to live in relationship with others.[13]

Amplified by Technology

Technology, as we've discussed already, helps you do work and solve problems. It's an incredible force—but it's just that, a force, for you to apply as you wish.

There's a well-known hierarchy in information science called the data-information-knowledge-wisdom hierarchy. Information is made up of connections between data, knowledge in connections between information, and wisdom in connections between knowledge. In many ways, the force of technology follows a similar progression. What it helps accomplish depends on the application and experience. Paper—one of the earliest technologies—has a different impact when used in scrolls than it does as origami, or after the advent of the printing press. Oil, used initially to produce kerosene for light and heat, is now used to make asphalt, wax, plastics, gasoline, and much more. And the internet, developed initially as a way for multiple computers to talk to each other, has changed everything about how we shop, communicate, and how our world functions.

Technology makes the world smaller and can make your impact so much larger. It gives you new windows into people and places, disseminates content more quickly and more widely, and provides immediate feedback from users or listeners. It can enable your impact to be shareable and repeatable, no longer a singular encounter or engagement, but something that can be accessed again. Others can connect to it, learn from it, and add to it over and over.

For the Sake of People

God's heart is for people. He wants us to know Him, to experience freedom, to live without fear of the world around us, and to remember that He's with us. Some of the most effective work you can do is work focused on others with empathy and care. People always matter in God's economy. Everything He does is focused on people. If we want to have an impact that lasts, we'll focus our work in the same way.

Impact taps into your purpose and where you fit in this unique time and place in our world. It requires being in relationship with others and belonging to communities because it encompasses more than your personal, individual work. Impact drives the solutions you develop as you collaborate with others and scale your vision. Scaling your impact is a direct result of collaboration as you invite others and leverage technology to share your solutions. None of us were created to live alone or serve alone. We're one body with many parts which are better together.

WHERE YOUR PASSION MEETS THE WORLD'S NEEDS

In one of our favorite books, notably called *Wishful Thinking*, Frederick Buechner writes that "the place God calls you to is the place where your deep gladness and the world's deep hunger meet."[14] We use this quote a lot because it's an important one. He was explaining what vocation is, and it wasn't necessarily about helping people think differently about God. In his role as a minister and writer, he describes the difference between vocation and a job and career, like this:

> There are all different kinds of voices calling you to all different kinds of work, and the problem is to find out which is the voice of God rather than of Society, say, or the Super-ego, or Self-Interest.
>
> By and large a good rule for finding out is this. The kind of work God usually calls you to is the kind of work (a) that you need most to do and (b) that the world most needs to have done.[15]

This definition of vocation is powerful because it helps us understand the connection between our passions—or our "deep gladness"—

and the world's needs. We all have some degree of purpose, no matter what we do or where we do it. Whether we're simply knowing God and making Him known or carrying out more uniquely personal purpose statements, our work is driven by what we need most to do or what the world needs most to have done.

Understanding your vocation is the key to a meaningful life because it answers two timeless questions: *Who am I?* and *Why am I here?* Answering that allows you to set the foundation for impact.

UNDERSTANDING THE WHY BEHIND YOUR MISSION STATEMENT

Most organizations, churches, and ministries have mission statements that define their why. They're usually concise and straightforward, aimed at sharing what they hope to accomplish. Mission statements are designed to articulate the purpose and answer the question about why the organization, church, or ministry exists in the first place. The best mission statements are the ones that are tied directly to the world's needs and also allow us to do what we most need to do.

The mission statement of World Vision is a good example. World Vision works "with the poor and oppressed to promote human transformation, seek justice and bear witness to the good news of the Kingdom of God."[16] Their leadership and staff includes all types of people, from all backgrounds, disciplines, and professions, who collaborate, design solutions, and scale the results, to ultimately impact the world.

If you're not sure what to do, start with the needs of the world. The world has *many* needs and is full of difficult, potentially life-changing problems. As we noted in chapter 7, of the significant issues we face in the world are distribution problems. Orphans need to find a family. The homeless need to find a home. The hungry need to find food. These issues feel so large and immovable; accordingly, there are simply not enough individuals working toward scalable, purposeful, and impactful solutions to them.

BUILDING CATHEDRALS

God calls some Christians to be pastors or ministry leaders, and others to be executives or entrepreneurs. Whatever your vocation is, it's ultimately about having an impact beyond yourself and your limited scope.

Have you ever heard the fable of the three bricklayers who all worked on the same wall in St. Paul's Cathedral? Architect Sir Christopher Wren, who was supervising the renovation, asked them, "What are you doing?" The first man replied, "I am laying bricks." The second bricklayer responded, "I am building a wall." But the third one answered, "I am building a great cathedral for God." The third worker saw a bigger picture—he understood how the simple, repetitive effort of laying bricks was more than that. He was able to tie what he was doing to the mission statement, which was to build a cathedral for God. He understood how he was having an impact. Even what some might consider the most insignificant job has meaning if you're able to see yourself as a cathedral builder, rather than a bricklayer.

One of the easiest places we start this conversation is with stay-at-home moms. When asked, they usually answer, "I'm taking care of babies . . . you know, laundry and diapers." We gently remind them of their real mission, and say, "You're raising little humans to be world changers." We've talked to workers about their jobs. Some say, "You know, I read email and go to meetings." It's a sure sign that they aren't thinking about the impact. We challenge them, "What if you're asking the key questions that change the current outdated approach and impact the lives of many?" Almost all of us get trapped in the mundane parts of our jobs sometimes and forget the big picture. Even church leaders are prone to feel caught up in the day-to-day and forget the impact they're making.

We love the story of President John F. Kennedy's first visit to a NASA center in 1962. He saw a janitorial worker off in the corner and walked over and introduced himself. "Hi, I'm Jack Kennedy. What are you doing?" The janitor replied, "Well, Mr. President, I'm helping put a man on the moon." When we see people answer the question not with the details of their daily tasks, but with the impact their work makes, we know they've grasped the possibilities of the future and have said yes to being part of it.

So, when people ask you what you're doing, what do you say? What impact is God calling you to have? What do you need to do to have an impact on the world? We encourage you to write it down on your Future Canvas worksheet.

COFFEE BEANS AND TRANSFORMATIONAL EXPERIENCES

Like many other books written these days, much of this one was crafted at Starbucks. Over cup after cup of coffee, we've contemplated how having a clearer understanding of our preferred future is like knowing the difference between acquiring a no-brand coffee bag or buying Starbucks coffee beans and creating a transformational cup of coffee. Let us explain.

Starbucks is a well-known industry leader, primarily because it's a company that's constantly transforming and reinventing itself. Although its mission is to be the "premier purveyor of the finest coffee in the world,"[17] its mission statement is more aspirational: "to inspire and nurture the human spirit—one person, one cup and one neighborhood at a time."[18] The impact Starbucks wants to have is to inspire and nurture the human spirit. Why? Because transformational experiences transform people! They take us somewhere we weren't on track for previously.

Memorable experiences lead to transformation. Starbucks realized this and therefore decided it wanted to be in the business of change. They can't just sell coffee beans because anyone can go to a local supermarket and buy a bag of them. They can't only procure and package coffee since there were already several other successful companies in that business. They can't just brew a cup of coffee and sell it to you because there are only so many cups of coffee that you can drink and so many coffee shops in the world. So Starbucks focused on the business of turning non-coffee drinkers into coffee aficionados. Their goal was to teach us to understand and appreciate coffee and desire more of it. They created space for communities to gather and allow transformation to happen. Coffee was just the excuse they gave us for coming together.

The best Starbucks baristas are the ones that serve you a cup of coffee, with a full understanding of the impact they're having, in pursuit of the preferred future Starbucks has set out to create. By moving beyond commodities, goods, and services to being in the business of transformational experiences, they've been able to increase the value rendered to their coffee-addicted customers.

But here's the question: How many of the baristas you interact with can tell you the mission statement of Starbucks? Most of them see it as a job, despite the lofty and aspirational mission statement to sell more coffee. And that's the difference between Starbucks and what you're doing. Coffee is great, but people understanding how they're part of creating transformation is even better.

Starbucks isn't the only company that understands they're in the business of creating transformation. Disney's theme parks are a good example. Walk into any of them, and you'll immediately see how the experience economy supplanted the service economy, which replaced the industrial economy. Today, we live in a world focused on transformation. Many interpret this as a focus on well-being and self-actualization; the experience economy focuses on meeting that (very personal) need.

THE ULTIMATE PURPOSE

As we talked about earlier in this chapter, as Christians, we're called to be imitators of God's purposes. Transformation is ultimately the business we're all in. Transformation is God's ultimate purpose both in us and through us, which means our vocation is to help others—and the world around us—be transformed. It's the reason He created us, and it signifies His intention to increase the impact He commands us to have. We're called to live this out in all aspects and stages of life, including work, friendship, marriage, parenthood, and with our customers.

When you understand this as a leader, it's no longer sufficient to design mediocre solutions that don't scale or meet an actual need. It doesn't work anymore to think small or just take care of your own. It's not enough to fly solo and avoid others. It's no longer sufficient to lead without a bold enough vision for where you're going.

There's power in the transformation process—and practice is the way you learn, one step at a time. Training is the school of transformation, and you grow and evolve as you gather, learn, and act. It rarely happens all at once, but is something you develop as you walk through life. It's something you understand better and value more with time.

Real impact comes from the execution of your vision as you keep your eyes fixed on the future God has set in your heart. The world yearns for the audacity of leaders with a better vision for the future, the heart to gather a crew and embark on an uncertain voyage, and the skill and courage to build a new rocket to get there. You possess an extraordinary opportunity to leave a lasting transformational impact on the world, and it's just a matter of getting started. What impact do you want to have? Take some time to write it down on your Future Canvas worksheet to capture it.

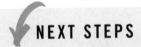

NEXT STEPS

1. Who has been a transformational leader in your life? What did you learn from them?

2. What's your passion? Where does it meet the world's needs and the needs of your community?

3. Where is a place you have had an impact in the past? Where is a place you currently have an impact? Is there something allowing that impact to happen?

4. Think about the impact you have had in the past, and that you're currently having. How can you continue to have that same impact in a changing environment? How can you make it more effective or more efficient on a larger scale?

5. What's the one thing you want to be said of you after your life is over?

PART 3:

FARSIGHTED

13

CURIOSITY IN ACTION

It's been said that vision without execution is a daydream, and execution without vision is a nightmare.[1]

—WILL MANCINI

Do you see better when you squint? Many of us who are physically nearsighted squint to improve our eyesight when looking farther away. This clarifies our vision through what's called the pinhole effect. The effect works by blocking out light coming from many different angles, and instead allowing only a few rays to enter. When you squint, your eye no longer needs to focus and refract so much light to create a clear and precise image. Instead, fewer beams project onto the retina at the back of the eye, and subsequently, your eye works less to see more. You can't squint all the time, though; it just strains your eyes. In the end, you need new lenses to correct the problem with your vision.

When it comes to the future, we're all born nearsighted. Our vision of what's next will always be blurry. It's just part of our human experience. Only God is omniscient. But you may not understand just *how* myopic you are until you start thinking about the future.

Like a corrective lens that you wear to improve your vision, the Futures Framework gives you clarity and strengthens your sight. In a world where there's more to see than ever before, looking through the eight lenses of the Futures Framework helps you determine where to focus. It limits the distractions around you and enables you to focus on the possibilities ahead so that you can see more clearly. It helps you actually become farsighted rather than compensating by squinting or rubbing your eyes.

Farsightedness is one of the essential qualities of a leader. Farsighted thinking is the ability to envision and articulate a future that's impactful and feasible. As a leader, you need to be able to articulate to others where you're headed, what's possible when you get there, and what you can accomplish by working together.

A farsighted vision—and ability to communicate it—has set apart some of the most effective and successful leaders of the last century. Martin Luther King was farsighted when he wrote his "I Have a Dream" speech. Walt Disney was farsighted when he envisioned Disneyland and later Disney World. Steve Jobs was farsighted when he pioneered the microcomputer. Bill Gates was farsighted when he worked toward putting a "computer on every desk and in every home."[2] John F. Kennedy was farsighted when he called NASA to put a man on the moon within a decade—and to do it before the Soviet Union did.[3] Ernest Shackleton was farsighted when he dreamed up his Antarctic expedition . . . and even more so when he continued forward toward rescue and didn't quit. Henry Ford was farsighted when he visualized a "motor car for the great multitude" that would provide "hours of pleasure in God's great open spaces."[4] Each of these leaders knew where they were headed, even though they may not have known how they were going to get there at the time. Having clarity about the future is powerful.

THE POWER OF A PREFERRED FUTURE

Two thousand years ago, as Jesus and His disciples were leaving Jericho, they encountered a blind man named Bartimaeus, who was sitting alongside the road begging. As they walked by, he shouted to Jesus, begging Him for help. Jesus stopped and called for Bartimaeus to come to Him. Without hesitation, Bartimaeus got up and came to Jesus. "What do you want me to do for you?" Jesus asked him. "Rabbi, I want to see," Bartimaeus answered—and Jesus healed him.[5] It was an incredible moment.

If Jesus asked you, "What do you want me to do for you?" would you know how to respond? What would you say? Do you have enough clarity on what you want and where you want to end up to ask Him for help?

Before Jesus even asked, Bartimaeus knew what preferred future he wanted. His clarity allowed him to ask the One who had the power to help him achieve it. In the process, he received even more than he could have conceived of in his blindness. Now that you have clarity on your preferred future, you are in a position to ask for help achieving it too.

ONLY GOD KNOWS HOW THE STORY ENDS

There are many possible futures that you can work toward, and it's your job as the leader to help discern which one is your *preferred* future. Which future aligns most clearly with your purpose, talents, gifts, and resources? Which future is most life-giving? Which future allows your organization, church, or ministry to have the most impact in your community and the world? Most importantly, as a Christian, toward which future do you believe God is calling you?

Now's a good time to remind you that your preferred future is only one of many possible futures. Your goal is to understand them to better discern and move toward where God's leading you. He's the only One who knows where the story ends and the best way to get there. So should you just give up and not think about the future? Not at all! God gives you the wisdom to discern your preferred future, the invitation to co-labor with Him, and the courage to do something about it.

Therefore, the essence of being a farsighted leader is having *enough* clarity about the future for you to know your direction in the present.

This doesn't mean you'll have all of the answers, or even most of the answers—or that you need to pretend you do. It merely means that you have clarity about which direction God's leading you.

As we talked about earlier, no matter how well you can describe your preferred future state, it's likely the reality of it will be different when you get to that moment in time. As God reminds Job, "Where were you when I laid the foundation of the earth? Tell me, if you have understanding" (Job 38:4). You aim for your preferred future, but you'll likely end up with an alternative future that you can't yet comprehend. It's a transformation process, and along the way, God transforms your perspective. He opens your eyes to a future of His choosing rather than your own.

HOW A PROPHET, PRIEST, AND KING FOUND THEMSELVES IN THE FRAMEWORK

We love to help leaders—and this includes you—identify their preferred futures. Over the years, we've helped both individuals and teams develop theirs as we've led them through the Futures Framework.

In several of the previous chapters, we introduced you to three of these leaders. You met Aaron, the entrepreneur of a start-up who used digital missions to reach the unchurched nones. There was also Tim, the pastor of a church who engaged his members in online small groups. Lastly, there was Lauren, the executive of a corporation who offered her team permanent remote work options. As you read about these leaders, you may not have realized that they align with the pastor, priest, and king examples we shared with you in chapter 5.

Let's take a look at each of these leaders and their preferred futures more closely. As we do, think about how you identify with one or more of them, as you see how they each formed their preferred future and now use it to create change and impact the world.

	ENTREPRENEUR	PASTOR	EXECUTIVE	YOU
IDENTITY (Chapter 5)	Identifies as a Prophet	Identifies as a Priest	Identifies as a King	
CONNECT (Chapter 6)	and connects with "unreached nones"	and connects with the congregants	and connects with the early-career employee	
BELONG (Chapter 7)	from around the world	in the local church	on a team	
GATHER (Chapter 8)	who met through digital missions.	that gather together in virtual small groups.	that meets together via remote work options.	
DESIGN (Chapter 9)	Using Lean Startup,	Using Human Centered Design,	Using Agile Development,	
COLLABORATE (Chapter 10)	collaborates with the Anglican Church in Iran	collaborates with other churches	collaborates with the tech industry	
SCALE (Chapter 11)	to scale to the MENA region	to scale to their city	to scale to the workforce at all life stages	
IMPACT (Chapter 12)	in order to share the gospel with every tribe, tongue, and nation.	in order to fulfill the Great Commission.	in order to create compelling media.	

Aaron the Entrepreneur

Digital missions, which is the idea that the online world is the biggest mission field in our era, got Aaron very excited. He was inspired that this strategy could help him reach the unchurched nones in his generation in a way in which others were unable. Aaron was living in a different country, which gave him a common starting point with those who felt out of place or disconnected.

While he wasn't a programmer, Aaron was a digital native who was super comfortable with technology and used it as a common language to build bridges with others. He had a passion for reaching those in his generation who were raised in the church but no longer affiliated with it. His preferred future was for his generation to reconnect with the church and their identity as Christians. He believed that digital missions was a unique and innovative way to make that happen globally. Aaron thought this preferred future was better than what currently existed and was eager to share it with others and begin to use it to have an impact. His core challenge was how to get people to share his vision and be engaged in it personally.

For Aaron, digital missions has taught him that the boundaries that divide most people can be overcome. As he now uses his preferred future vision statement to guide him, he knows that he can find a sense of belonging with his generation as they continue to gather online. He develops his approach to digital missions in short, rapid cycles that are deeply connected to the communities around the world. It allows them to share their feedback and unique cultural views that shape the approach. Every time the community gathers—both in-person and online—they bring their incredible gifts to bear on an evangelistic mission that very few of them were part of locally.

Tim the Pastor

As a pastor, Tim highly valued helping his church members develop real-life, authentic relationships. Yet he understood that where and how people gathered together could vary to better accommodate the demands of jobs, parenting needs, or other life situations. Tim knew that how his community gathered could include an online option, but he needed to determine how to implement changes without forfeiting a genuine connection.

Tim's preferred future was for every person in his church to be connected in an authentic community, and he was willing to change some of the practices and methods to make that happen. He also saw how this change could help not only his church members but others in his city. His core challenge was how to manage the change at a speed that would pull everyone in, from early adopter to staunch traditionalist, and not lose the connection they already had with each other.

As a result of developing his preferred future, Tim now has a clearer vision of how to connect with his congregation and help them connect. Tim's innovations, which started with a better virtual small group experience, quickly grew to include a new virtual church platform that not only broadcast their Sunday service messages but engaged those attending in an entirely new way. Tim's congregation is still able to experience authentic community because Tim has helped them recognize how they can better belong together in both the digital and analog world. This has attracted new members in the community who didn't traditionally attend church and have new ideas on how to improve the experience for others like them. These fresh perspectives have continued to fuel the transformation both inside the church as well as his city.

Tim also noticed that as his congregants now feel more valued and are developing a growing interest in what the church has to say to them. They aren't opting out of "regular" church because of the virtual option. Instead, they're filling the gaps with it when life necessitates, and it's increasing their commitment overall. As this approach continues to be successful, Tim stays focused on the humans in the process: how they gather, what they need, and the realities of their lives. He's also seen other churches express interest and has been able to share these strategies so that they can collaborate to reach the entire city.

Lauren the Executive

One of Lauren's strengths as a leader was that she genuinely cared about the people on her team. She knew that they were her greatest resource. Her preferred future focused on scaling her company's ability to fulfill its core mission over the long term. She saw some success, but it wasn't as widespread as she wanted. There were pockets of dissension that had built up over a transitional season.

Lauren's core challenge wasn't related to their product—which was doing fine—but to the business process and how her team functioned within the organization. She needed to reconnect them with the vision and reengage them directly in the core mission. As a result of identifying her preferred future, she started by connecting with her newer, early-career employees. They were looking for ways to work remotely because they had an expectation for work and life not just to be balanced but to support each other. While this challenged Lauren's work preferences, her willingness to adapt to their needs increased their commitment.

As the way they work together has changed, the team has grown closer and now operates more effectively. Lauren continues to let the strategy evolve as they design it together. She's also had technology companies approach her to partner and help expand the work of the company. What started with a relatively small change by Lauren led to her team feeling reinvigorated because they were able to effectively contribute and have a collective, measurable impact, no matter where in the world they were working from.

You

What about you? What's the preferred future you've developed in the past eight chapters? Once you know that, you can develop a plan to work toward that vision. You don't have to accept whatever future comes along. You're a creator and a world changer who's made in the image of God.

- You choose what your identity is (and ignore the ways culture tries to define you).

- You decide where to connect with others in relationship in light of that identity.

- You find where you belong, which leads to where you gather.

- You design a way to solve the problems and address the needs you see around you.

- You then collaborate with others to scale your vision to have an impact.

If you're still defining your preferred future and analyzing what you can do about it, here are some more questions you can ask yourself:

- What technology do I need to achieve my preferred future? What technology might disrupt this approach?

- What are the habits, preferences, and expectations of people that I need to change to achieve my preferred future? What might disrupt this approach?

- How might my current mission change to achieve my preferred future? How can I be more specific in describing our mission or better describe our problem, which will help lead to actionable steps forward?

- How will the space within which we operate support our ability to achieve my preferred future? Can I identify any unexpected changes to how space is used, either physically or virtually, that will disrupt our current approach?

GETTING STARTED

When it comes to your preferred future, your primary responsibility is to have faith and get started. Begin by writing it down, visualizing it, and sharing it with others.

Write Your Preferred Future Down

Over the past eight chapters, we've encouraged you to write down your preferred future one lens of the Futures Framework at a time. You started by contemplating your identity and finished by envisioning your impact. With each chapter, you've come closer and closer to defining and capturing your preferred future concisely and clearly. By now, you have most likely developed your preferred vision statement. If you haven't, take a few moments to look back over your notes and continue working on it.

Visualize Your Preferred Future

Visualization is a method to help bring your vision to life. Microsoft is a company that does this well. It's known for its physical showrooms, powered by cutting-edge technology, which demonstrate what the home and office of the future might look like.[6] By constructing proto-types, Microsoft gives clients the ability to test out the concepts that are informed by the latest research and development. This lets Microsoft kick-start conversations about how these potentially transformative solutions could help them meet their goals.

After writing down your preferred vision statement, you can use visualization by developing narratives to test assumptions, challenge thinking, and rehearse the implications. You do this by placing yourself in the shoes of someone living in that future and imagining what it would be like to experience your vision.

Share Your Preferred Future with Others

Have you ever played the game Mad Libs? In it, you have a story with blank spaces for you to fill in with specific parts of speech such as nouns, adjectives, and exclamations. One of the players silently reads the story and knows the context for each word. It's this player who prompts the other players to provide words to fill in the blanks. After all the words are added, the comical story is read aloud. You can use a form of Mad Libs to start a conversation about the future with your team. Our version of the game will leave you and your team feeling inspired.

In the future:

How do you identify yourself? _____ (noun)

Who do you want to connect to in a relationship? _____ (person)

What communities do you want to belong to? _____ (group)

Where do you want to gather? _____ (place)

What do you want to create? _____ (noun)

Who can you collaborate with? _____ (person or group or organization)

How can you scale using technology? _____ (noun)

What impact do you want to have? _____ (result)

The ability to communicate your preferred future simply and inclusively is how farsighted leaders invite others to join the journey.

ENJOYING THE PROCESS

When Ali was a kid, her most-wished-for superpower was teleportation. Travel meant packing, long car rides where she often got sick, and frequent distractions and pit stops along the way. She was tired of it all and longed to reach destinations instantly. As you look to your preferred future, you might relate. You may be thinking how nice it would be to enlist a superpower just to fast-forward you to that future. Unfortunately, this book can't help you with that.

The preferred future you've written down and shared with others isn't going to happen overnight. It's a process, and the process is hard. Most of us are impatient and prefer instant change. It can be frustrating to have clarity about a better and impact-filled future that God's calling you to, but not be able to see it realized immediately. When you understand firsthand how long the journey might be, you may start to wonder if it's worth it and if you want it that much. But it's during this journey that you'll pick up additional insights you'll need for when you do finally arrive at your destination.

Remember, God gives you the wisdom to discern your preferred future and the courage to pursue it. As we reach the end of this chapter, you may know where you're headed. You may have a clear vision for the future and are ready to get started. But it's also possible you still feel unclear, or you're still exploring the future as you map out possible futures and work through the Futures Framework. Whatever the case is, we encourage you to stick with us, no matter how daunting it may feel. In the next chapter, we'll give you a five-step process to help you achieve your preferred future.

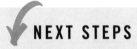

NEXT STEPS

1. Who is the most farsighted leader you've encountered? What was it like to work with them?

2. What can you not see right now, but wish you could?

3. What's the preferred future that you've constructed as you've worked through the book?

4. Is that future achievable on your own? Where does it need God to show up to make it possible?

5. Who do you need to share it with to get their perspective or feedback?

14

PAPER ROCKETS

Your task is not to foresee [the future], but to enable it.[1]

—ANTOINE DE SAINT-EXUPÉRY

NASA has designed many paper rockets throughout its history. One of the first paper rockets we helped create was in 2004. The President of the United States had just announced a bold new vision to return to the moon. We were on one of the original design teams to develop a modern lunar architecture. It was a plan for how to launch humans to the moon, build a lunar base, colonize the moon, and use it as a springboard to Mars.

Engineers from every discipline contributed to the design of this lunar mission that would return humans to the moon, but this time to stay. With precision, we calculated how many individual rocket launches and resupply missions it would take to get us there. We crafted the critical building blocks of a lunar base, as well as strategized the best way to permanently colonize the moon to prepare for humanity's eventual journey to Mars.

Our plan was visionary, affordable, and, most importantly, very doable. The problem is, we never actually did it. Instead, like many paper rockets designed before this one, it was placed on a dusty shelf in the backroom of a 1960s-era government office building. The hope was that one day a future generation would have not only the vision for exploration but also the tenacity to achieve it.

This paper rocket isn't the only one to be shelved. Very few of these aspirational visions turn into impactful solutions that change our world. Most of them are simply thoughtful words scribed onto paper, rolled into a tube, and set on fire. Okay, not literally set on fire, but they might as well be because they're put on a shelf and forgotten. There are a few, though, that turn into reality. You probably know about them because they're the ones that inspire awe and wonder—like the crane that lowered a car-sized rover onto Mars, or the International Space Station and the new rockets being built today.

The reason that many grand visions never turn into anything other than gravitationally challenged paper studies isn't that the idea itself was flawed, but because the will to implement the vision wasn't there. The only difference between paper rockets and actual rockets is that it takes someone with vision *and* the willingness to keep trying until they reach their goal. It's not enough to have a great idea. You have to actually launch it.

Having a clear vision for what you want to achieve is the first step on your journey to success. What you do next is up to you. We've worked with a lot of "ideas" people throughout our careers. They're useful at developing concepts and even inspiring a workforce. The theories behind their ideas might even be plausible, but they ultimately fail because the leaders in charge of the mission didn't have the tenacity to see it through to the end. We want to teach you how not to make the same mistake because when you build your rocket, you'd probably prefer that it launches.

FIVE STEPS TO IMPLEMENT YOUR PREFERRED FUTURE

Over the years, we've designed a lot of paper rockets. Each one has made us better consultants, strategists, technologists, and innovators. And, along the way, we've learned what it takes to launch one—and that's strategy. The paper rocket that is your preferred future can only be achieved through careful planning and intentional action. A strategy is a critical bridge between this present and that future.

Turning your preferred future into an actionable plan can be complex, potentially risky, and riddled with points of possible breakdown. But that's why we're here. We want to help you by giving you a systematic approach you can use to transform your future. This approach is summed up in a practical five-step process:

1. Determine the current "as-is" state of your organization through an assessment.

2. Identify your strengths, weaknesses, opportunities, and threats by considering the forces changing the world around you.

3. Identify the barriers that currently hold you back.

4. Reframe your approach by using the Futures Framework.

5. Prioritize the top recommendations through a collaborative discussion with your leadership team.

1. Assess Your Current State

Do you remember how we talked about your "as-is" state in chapter 5? Well, before you can develop a strategy and start working toward your preferred future, you need to take the pulse of the current state of your organization, church, or ministry. You want to have a comprehensive understanding of this because how others imagine the future—or hold onto the past—can influence their collective attitudes, behaviors, and decisions.

The chances are that your organization, church, or ministry is currently operating with outdated assumptions, beliefs, attitudes, and practices, which have been codified in your operational model over years of success. These choices likely are reflected throughout your culture. The choices and actions you make today ultimately shape how the future actually unfolds. This is why it's critical to understand what perceptions exist that limit or constrain you and your team from moving forward.

In chapters 6 and 9, we discussed the importance of empathy. Developing a sense of how those you lead think, feel, behave, and want is vital to assess your current "as-is" state. It also helps you become aware of how the future is seen from their perspective. Change, particularly more transformational and radical change, can be uncomfortable. Thinking beyond how business or ministry has always been done is difficult. It can cause some individuals to incorrectly interpret the future as a shinier version of the past. Empathy lets you gain insight into what they believe to be true today, what they need to help them understand the preferred future you envision, and what might hold them back from coming alongside you to realize it.

While there are many approaches you could use to develop empathy and understand the current state, we recommend a simple assessment to gauge the climate and readiness for change and innovation. This assessment can be as simple as sending out a survey to your leadership team. We often start every conversation with our clients with a climate assessment survey that includes these twelve questions:

1. How connected do you feel to the current mission and vision of your ministry or business?

2. What individuals or organizations are driving change in your industry right now? Why?

3. How did you lead your community to where you are today?

4. How do you currently innovate? What works and what doesn't?

5. How could you innovate in the future?

6. Where do you see innovation currently happening?

7. What do you see as the barriers to innovation?

8. What are two or three particular strengths your team or group brings to the table when it comes to positioning yourselves well for the future?

9. If you could hire three more people, what unconventional skills would they have, and why?

10. Which parts of your job would you like to kill or eliminate?

11. What "next step" would you like to see taken to encourage a culture of innovation?

12. How optimistic are you about the future of your organization and your ability to implement that mission?

2. Understand Your Strengths, Weakness, Opportunities, and Threats

Once you've conducted a survey, we recommend performing a classic SWOT analysis. SWOT stands for Strengths, Weaknesses, Opportunities, and Threats. Strengths and weaknesses are those internal factors over which you have some control and can change. Opportunities and threats are external elements that are happening outside your organization, church, or ministry. Threats are real—the key is putting them in perspective in the context of your strengths, weaknesses, and opportunities. A SWOT analysis helps you place these things into an organized list.

STRENGTH	WEAKNESS	OPPORTUNITY	THREAT
Things your organization does really well	Things your organization does poorly	Clear areas where you could make a difference with little effort	Emerging competitors
Qualities that separate you from your competitors	Things your competitors do faster or cheaper or better	An emerging need that has been identified	Changing regulatory, legal, or political environments
Places that you operate well in	Resources that you lack	Perceptions others have of what you should be doing but are not already doing	Negative press coverage or social media discussion
Resources that you have, such as people and technology	Unclear expectations or value propositions		Changing attitudes and expectations

While a classical SWOT analysis is helpful, we recommend modifying the approach to align it with the Futures Framework better. This modified method allows you to consider your strengths, weaknesses, opportunities, and threats in relation to the four forces we introduced in chapter 3. It also helps you organize the insights according to the Futures Framework. To do this, create a grid with the SWOT categories across the top x-axis and the four forces from the Futures Framework across the vertical y-axis. You can also download a template to use from futuresframework.com.

	STRENGTH	WEAKNESS	OPPORTUNITY	THREAT
PURPOSE		Not everyone understands where we are going or why we do what we do.		
PEOPLE	We already have really talented people!			
PLACE			We could use technology to reach people in digital spaces.	
TECH				We may be disrupted by a new church startup that has just opened its doors down the road.

The analysis will help you uncover many useful insights. What are the current beliefs about the forces of purpose, people, place, and technology? What are the obvious changes you anticipate from each of these four forces? What makes you uncomfortable and keeps you up at night when you consider these forces? Maybe it's the rapid rate of technological change, the shifting demographics in the workforce, the transition from the physical to a digital world, or a rudderless purpose that's no longer firmly guiding your organization, church, or ministry. By recognizing your current assumptions and beliefs about how each of the forces influences your world, you'll start to uncover real barriers that may be holding you back. Futures thinking encourages you to think differently by intentionally challenging your assumptions and mindsets.

3. Identify the Barriers to Innovation

Many leaders never move past the paper rocket stage because they experience internal barriers that don't allow their vision to take root or do well. A barrier, by definition, is an obstacle that prevents success. After you've assessed your current culture and how it affects all members of your team or community, the next step is to analyze your feedback regarding the current innovation climate and identify the barriers that can hold you back.

Identifying your barriers to innovation is often a challenge to do. The barriers themselves might not be explicitly obvious, and even if they are, you may not recognize them as a significant threat to your future. Some barriers to innovation are disguised as strengths. But, without identifying the barriers to innovation, efforts to focus on the future will likely serve to reinforce current logic and business as usual. Once you identify these barriers, you can start to eliminate or overcome them.

Back in 2008, YouVersion's Bible app was born out of both recognizing barriers and a willingness to respond to them rather than merely react. Craig Groeschel and the leadership of Life Church placed a high value on ending Bible poverty. They discussed ways to use Facebook or YouTube to address this issue, but none of them were excited about these options. Few in their circles were using those technologies them-selves yet, and they didn't know what to do with the incipient launch of the Apple App Store. One member of their church said, "How hard could this be?" and built the first version of the Bible app. It became one of the first 200 free apps Apple offered, and now, a third of a *billion* people have downloaded it. It's changed the way people interact with the Bible. Many roadblocks could have prevented this revolution from happening:

We don't use that, so surely other people won't either.

No, we don't have time to experiment with new approaches.

Will apps really matter anyway? And they're probably too hard to create.

The Bible is too precious to put online! It's about the book!

Smartphones won't be that popular. Maybe we just need a website.

There were many opportunities to say no. But because the leaders said yes and were willing to challenge their assumptions and potentially fail, they succeeded instead. Their preferred future—where everyone had access to Scripture—was fulfilled in a different way and on a dif-ferent timeline than they imagined, but it was achieved.

Take a look at the SWOT analysis you did and circle the items that stand out to you as barriers. Review your strengths and weaknesses to identify those things you have some control over and can change. Review the opportunities and threats that are external to your orga-nization, church, or ministry to see what you might be able to take advantage of or protect against.

In our work with leaders, when we consider their strengths, weak-nesses, opportunities, and threats in relationship with the four forces in our framework, we see seven common barriers. They appear repeatedly and hinder the organizations, churches, and ministries we work with from realizing their preferred future:

- **Vision:** a lack of vision or direction

- **Structure:** inertia, bureaucracy, silos, overlaps, or gaps

- **Leadership:** lack of confident leadership

- **Resources:** lack of time, funding, and talent

- **Processes:** lack of processes or systems

- **Culture:** lack of trust, deeply rooted risk aversion, and/or a fear of failure

- **Diversity:** limited diversity in background, approach, perspective, or expertise, especially in how problems are solved

4. Reframe Using the Futures Framework

Now that you've identified the barriers that keep you from innovating and realizing your preferred future, you can start to develop a strategy. Using the Futures Framework, create another grid. This time, list out the barriers to innovation across the top x-axis and along the y-axis, write out the eight elements of the Futures Framework.

This grid allows you to systematically address the barriers that are holding you back in context with the preferred future you're trying to achieve. In the last nine chapters, you identified your preferred future statement. Now we want you to dissect each part of that statement and consider what's holding you back.

Assuming you use the seven categories of barriers we proposed in step three, there are fifty-six boxes on the grid. Your goal is to identify one action item for each of these boxes. For example, if you've identified the lack of leadership as a barrier to innovation, it might be appropriate to identify an executive leader in your organization, church, or ministry who's responsible for championing innovation. The work of reframing is like that of a heart surgeon. It's hard, the hours are long, and the learning curve is steeper than Mount Everest. But the result will be a comprehensive list of recommendations that serves as the building blocks of your implementation strategy.

	VISION	STRUCTURE	LEADERSHIP	RESOURCES	PROCESSES	CULTURE	DIVERSITY
IDENTIFY		Assess current organizational strucure					
RELATE			Create new channels for engagement				Regularly poll for member and community perceptions
BELONG							
GATHER					Identify needs in the city and community		
DESIGN				Create virtual opportunities for regular events		Hold first all-virtual gathering	
COLLABORATE	Provide ways for all staff to give input						
SCALE							
IMPACT							

5. Prioritize the Top Seven Actions

At this point in the process, many of the leaders we work with feel overwhelmed. They appreciate the clarity they have now with their preferred future and express a willingness to lean in and do the hard work to achieve it. They've even had honest and open conversations with their teams about the barriers that are holding them back. But many of them still feel like knowing what to do next isn't clear. We tell them that the essence of a great strategy is choosing what not to do (because you can't do everything)!

Once you recognize that you don't have unlimited time or resources, the last step is to review the recommendations from step four and prioritize them into a near-term action plan. We suggest identifying one from each of the vertical columns. For each column, consider the first or the most effective action you can take to address the barrier that's holding you back. Prioritization may require establishing rating criteria and a scale to measure the impact or feasibility. It also depends on your future goals and, therefore, should be closely tied to your preferred future and not just your mission and objectives.

The result is a prioritized, actionable, realistic, and visionary plan for the future. The seven actions you identify are where you can start. These actions address the seven barriers to innovation and start you along the journey to realizing your preferred future. With this approach comes the ability to apply the framework to your situation and develop targeted recommendations that can be used to build your strategy.

PUTTING IT ALL TOGETHER AS THE INGREDIENTS FOR A STRATEGY

As a leader, these five steps are the most important things you can do now that you have clarity on your preferred future and where you're going. These recommendations are the ingredients for a strategy. The outcome of working systematically through them is you'll gain specific suggestions and a prioritized action plan that will set you on the right course.

We've found that the organizations, churches, and ministries who achieve the most from our Futures Framework are the ones who institutionalize the process, develop their own tailored and actionable strategy, and use it to inform decisions at all levels. To help give you a better sense of what this looks like in action, we want to introduce you to a local pastor we worked with recently. Let's consider his preferred future and walk through the five steps to show you how it works.

This pastor imagined a future where his church was more effectively reaching a younger generation through digital missions. With his vision for a better future in hand, he quickly started to implement it. First, he polled his leadership team, staff, key volunteers, and a sample population from his congregation, to determine the current climate within his church. Additionally, he held a half-day retreat with his leadership team to share the results of the Futures Framework. He invited others to consider the effect of the four forces and develop a SWOT analysis for their church. The results looked something like this:

While the pastor was surprised by some of the findings, he wasn't by others. His church had successfully grown from a small church plant a decade earlier into what's considered a megachurch today. Many of the factors that made them a successful startup had become key components of the church's culture. After the half-day retreat, the pastor worked with a small volunteer strategy team to analyze the results and identify the barriers that were keeping them from realizing their vision.

- **Vision**: We lack a defined vision for how we are going to reach a younger generation that is not attending church.
- **Structure**: We are currently not structured well to experiment with new approaches.
- **Leadership**: We don't have anyone on the leadership team with expertise in digital missions.
- **Resources**: We have not allocated resources (time or funding) to start a new ministry.
- **Processes**: All of our processes assume we meet only on Sundays in a physical building.

- **Culture**: Our organization has a hard time changing.
- **Diversity**: We are unable to reach a younger generation, especially among minority populations.

	STRENGTH	WEAKNESS	OPPORTUNITY	THREAT
PURPOSE	We have a really clear mission statement.	Not everyone understands where we are going or why we do what we do.	We could clarify our strategy and prioritize innovation.	Church attendance, especially among a younger generation, is declining.
PEOPLE	Our staff and congregation is really ready for a change!	We are not structured well to be flexible and nimble and take advantage of new opportunities.	We should recruit top talent with expertise in using technology to reach a younger generation.	We have a culture of niceness that makes hard conversations difficult.
PLACE	We are a recognized leader in our area and are well placed geographically to reach our community.	We lack success planning and have a fear of failure.	We have not considered ways to expand our presence outside of our physical location.	We do not have expertise in how to reach our community well.
TECH	We already have the technology we need to start a digital campus and to influence through social media.	We do not understand what data we own or have access to, or how to use the data we have.	We could improve our IT services group and recruit more volunteers with digital expertise.	We may be disrupted by a new church start-up that has just opened its doors down the road.

Nobody disagreed with the barriers; they were all fairly obvious. The majority of the discussion at the next leadership meeting focused on how to address the obstacles. They looked at how to disrupt the church in a positive way to help realize the preferred future of better connecting the congregation in authentic community using digital technology. Over a few weeks, the team identified something for every one of the boxes on the grid. In some cases, the recommendations related to a change in the practices or methods. In other cases, the suggestions alluded to core structural changes the church needed to make.

During the final futures meeting, the pastor reminded everyone on the leadership team that the most important thing they could do was to start executing the vision. To do that, they needed to consider what to do right now with limited time and resources. As a team, they identified seven actions to start immediately and assigned one team member the responsibility for implementing the action.

The pastor and his team committed to spending more time to further organize the remaining action items from the Futures Framework into a long-term strategy to incrementally and intentionally work toward their preferred future. This strategy included goals, objectives, and plans and led to specific decisions and activities to undertake. The leadership team measured their progress over time and continued to revisit their strategy to determine its effectiveness and make course corrections as needed.

THE DREAMS THAT LIVE

Do you remember Shackleton and his voyage to Antarctica? It's rumored that he placed an advertisement for crewmates in the London newspaper *The Times*.[2] It's said to have read: "Men wanted for hazardous journey. Low wages, bitter cold, long hours of complete darkness. Safe return doubtful. Honour and recognition in event of success."[3] While it's argued this ad is a myth, not fact, it reminds us that Shackleton's voyage could have stayed a theory, the blue-sky dream of a reckless man. But he didn't give in or give up when others scoffed. He wasn't afraid of hard work or risk. Whether it was through an ad or other means, he found the right people to bring on the voyage with him.

Think back to Walt Disney and his dream of building a theme park. When this dream became a reality and Disneyland opened on July 17, 1955, his dedication read: "To all who come to this happy place: Welcome. Disneyland is your land. Here age relives fond memories of the past . . . and here youth may savor the challenge and promise of the future. Disneyland is dedicated to the ideals, the dreams, and the

	VISION	STRUCTURE	LEADERSHIP	RESOURCES	PROCESSES	CULTURE	DIVERSITY
IDENTIFY	Identify community and mission field	Assess current organizational strucure	Identify and hire a digital campus pastor	Set aside funding to support digital outreach	Create a cybersecurity process to protect identity	Assess online persona and values	Assess virtual audience and potential
RELATE	Gather feedback on virtual platform with stakeholders	Create a ministry for digital missions	Create new channels for engagement	Hire a technologist to build a digital infrastructure	Use online tools to chat to connect anytime & anywhere	Address isolation and territorialism	Regularly poll for member and community perceptions
BELONG	Find which communities are already virtual and seek input	Identify places of virtual intersection	Find digital natives in church community	Identify and prioritize digital channels	Identify needs in the city and community	Build bridges across silos in community	Develop diverse partners locally
GATHER	Hold regular online office hours	Go as multi-channel as possible	Include top leaders in virtual engagement	Create virtual opportunities for regular events	Develop tutorials to get online easily	Hold first all-virtual gathering	Invite community to speak into process
DESIGN	Develop a common language around innovation	Whiteboard new community structures	Hire for digital skills and experience	Digitize existing resources and content	Priortize needs and resources	Hold a design thinking session	Regularly engage nonmembers
COLLABORATE	Provide ways for all staff to provide input	Consider rotational opportunities	Benchmark with other successful ministries	Work with churches from other demographics	Cross-pollinate with other ministries	Evaluate where you can celebrate other cultures	Find new content partners
SCALE	Develop a vision statement for the community	Plant new efforts with additional leaders	Commission church members for online outreach	Leverage global gifts and expertise	Develop a framework for virtual ministry	Allow for diversity of culture	Use social media platforms to reach new audiences
IMPACT	Communicate the success stories	Measure to metrics and adjust as needed	Consider succession planning	Evaluate ROI annually and communicate	Create metrics to measure progress	Share spinoffs and success stories	Activate whole church to serve

hard facts that have created America . . . with the hope that it will be a source of joy and inspiration to all the world."[4] Originally, people had laughed at his idea because Disney was an animator. But he wasn't dissuaded. With a childlike curiosity, he engaged others who shared his vision because he knew the future they could make together was far better than any he could make alone.

Remember the International Space Apps Challenge? We had a dream to engage everyone on Earth to contribute tangibly to space exploration, so we created a place to make that possible. Many thought it wasn't doable, or too complex, or that people didn't have anything to contribute (since this was rocket science, after all). But we couldn't imagine a world *without* all of these amazing contributors, who did things NASA couldn't do on their own.

Not all of the rockets that became more than a stack of paper were necessarily successful because they were the best rockets. After all, there are many different ways to design a rocket to accomplish the same objective. These missions were successful because the leaders who envisioned them held onto their visions. They didn't allow the naysayers, the barriers, or the fear to stand in their way. Many of us think that's a rare skill or spiritual gift that's bestowed serendipitously, but it's not. The reality is that it's a process and a discipline that requires humility, prayer, and reverent submission to a trustworthy God who invites us to join Him in impacting our world—an opportunity that is available to us all.

NEXT STEPS

1. What vision do you have for your life or your organization, church, or ministry that's been relegated to a drawer? How did it end up there?

2. Who are your "users" that you are targeting? They could be your audience, community, members, or potential customers. What makes them unique? What do they care about?

3. What are your strengths? Weaknesses? Opportunities? Threats?

4. What are the barriers that are holding you back from your vision?

5. What do you think the first priority next step is?

15

INFINITE POSSIBILITIES

But, as it is written, "What no eye has seen, nor ear heard,
nor the heart of man imagined, what God has prepared
for those who love him."

—1 CORINTHIANS 2:9

We love a good adventure. Between the two of us, we've driven race cars, jumped out of planes, and dived to the depths of the ocean. We've traveled around the globe, helped restore communities after massive disasters, and walked through war zones.

Having been on many adventures, we can tell you that the journey through the unknown is the best way to grow as human beings. It's where we discover what we're made of and what God has prepared for us. It's where we find the stories that haven't been told, the possibilities that haven't been discovered, and the views that we haven't yet seen. Choosing to go on an adventure is deciding to think outside of the walls of safety and experience something more. It's a risk—but it's a risk worth taking. Not going would result in certain stagnation, and likely regret, over all the might-have-beens.

Going on an adventure requires being brave, overcoming your fears, and permitting yourself to take the first step. After reading this book, you're now better equipped to think about what comes next and ready to step into the unknown. But for those around you who haven't read this book, this can all sound scary. Remember, most people don't like disruption and change. Ambiguity is frustrating, and like Peter stepping out on the boat to walk toward Jesus on the water, it's easy to get distracted by the waves.[1] It's a challenge to get past the inner dialogue that whispers, "I can't walk on water."

When you're the one with a vision for a better future, you can quickly feel like an outsider in your organization, church, or ministry. You can become exhausted trying to resolve the tension between getting unstuck from the status quo and getting started on the journey ahead. There will be people who won't understand the need for change or the urgency for it. They will prefer the past that they can see and touch over the uncertain future. Many organizations, churches, and ministries get the planning right, have a well-researched strategy, attract great leaders, and have a sustainable approach for innovation, but fail to prepare their teams for the hard choices ahead. This requires trust.

Trust is the currency of innovation. The very nature of innovation requires that teams are willing to try something new and are open to the potential for failure. Carey Nieuwhof writes, "When trust is high, the speed of getting things done rises (sometimes exponentially) and costs decrease."[2]

It's also a personal, human quality that needs ongoing attention. Trust requires growth and learning, and when it's violated necessitates conflict and reconciliation. Without it, your team will never go beyond its job description. You will not lead your industry, nor will you change the world.

As you get ready to disrupt the status quo, sail the uncharted seas, and aim to leave a lasting impact for generations to come, start by building trust with your team so that together you can take the first step and push away from the shoreline. To do this, you must go first in asking the hard questions, exploring the answers, and being willing to take some risk. Taking risks means that you need to acknowledge that you discover what comes next by experience—and that often things don't always work how you might expect. It gives you chances to confront your natural fear of failure.

Paul's reminder "to live is Christ, to die is gain" (Phil. 1:21) frames the idea of building trust and taking a risk in an eternal perspective, acknowledging that you are set free to explore the future because you have nothing to lose. Paul invites you to put your trust in God and take a risk to journey with Him toward what He's already prepared for you. You are free to trust in Him because what matters most is already secure. It's only when you consider what happens next that you discover how far it's possible to go.

Acknowledgments

When we were children, we didn't understand why a few people would remain in their seats to sit through the never-ending rolling credits at the end of movies. Some of the credits were so long that if we would have left the theater when they started, we would have been home by the time they ended. So, why would anyone stick around?

It took decades of watching countless superhero films for us to really appreciate the credits. You may have noticed that films like Marvel's *Captain America: The Winter Soldier*, entice you with "post-credit scenes" that often reveal hidden additional pieces of a puzzle. The post-credit scenes might make you laugh, teach you something new, or tease you with a clue about an upcoming sequel.

Over the years, as theaters emptied around us, we started to pay attention to the names that scrolled across the screen in between the post-credit scenes. The credits were usually scrolling so fast that we couldn't catch the names of every single person, but what was clear is that it takes an endless cast and crew of talented people to create a body of work that inspires, educates, and entertains us.

Sir Isaac Newton understood this well. As the scientist who first identified the effects of gravity, he knew that his discoveries about the universe were only made possible in the light of the contributions of others. He sums it up well when he wrote a now-renowned line in a letter to his rival Robert Hooke in 1676: "If I have seen further it is by standing on the shoulders of giants."[1]

A book like this could never have been written alone. We have been fortunate to stand on the shoulders of giants. Thank you to each of you who have been a part of this adventure. So many have influenced this book, and it's impossible to capture every name in the quickly scrolling credits, but we see your imprint on nearly every page of this book.

Thank you to Asher, Kai, and Adah, who loaned their Daddy out so many weekends to collaborate with Ms. Ali over countless cups of coffee. We really wish we would have bought some Starbucks stock instead of all those cups of caffeine. Thank you to Krista for loving us well, and supporting us in this adventure, through all the small, unnoticed things you do every day.

Throughout our lives, there have been a few who have so influenced our thinking and the trajectory of our lives—the true giants—that we simply would not exist without them. To Vicky and Bob Dresser, for taking a young impressionable and lost soul under their wing and teaching him what the love of Jesus looks like through the way you live your lives. To Pat and David Knox, for praying for your future son-in-law from before the time your daughter was even born. To Margaret Newton, for teaching a young and inexperienced believer how leadership starts with friendship and fellowship. To Ruthie Weller, for helping one woman believe her voice had value. To Tim and Kristi, who model leadership that looks like Jesus, even in the desert of the Middle East, you are incredible examples of so many of these principles. To Cyndi Whitecotton, who is one of our favorite thinking partners about futures. To our original OpenGov team, who believed in that Space Apps dream, and committed to making meaningful participation in exploration possible for anyone anywhere. To Yuri and Cosmo, for being the ones who gave us our first chance to work together.

We want to particularly thank, by name, all of you who willingly invested your time and talent to help review, edit, and contribute to early versions of this book. We are forever grateful to you. To Charlie Auvermann, Cyndi Whitecotton, Stacy Morgan, Brian Schoening, Allison Swenson, Britt Tucker, Wendy Scott, Josie Decker, Jonelle Tucker, Steven Gonzales, Raph Neighbour, Marcia Griffin, Brent Fiechtner, Greg Oliver, Jonathan Ridenour, Aaron Chester, Michael Leyva, Rachel Matthys, Ryan Lehtinen, and Alan Mason: you each shaped the words, stories, and examples through your invaluable comments, conversations, and contributions. The book is so much better for it, and we are better for it.

Of course, we would not even be here without the future that both sets of our parents ushered in for us. Thank you for being our guides and helping us navigate life's uncharted waters.

Finally, we want to thank the incredible team at Moody Publishers who believed in us and provided outstanding support along the way. To Amy Simpson, for asking a question after our presentation at a missions conference that led directly to this work. To Amy again (you get two mentions for all of your support), for helping us navigate the publishing and editing process. To Ashleigh Slater, who improved this book by a factor of a zillion (which is technically defined as "an indeterminately large number"). To all the others on the team . . . like the astronauts who are the faces of the mission and the ones in all the pictures, our names are on the book, but you helped build the rocket, and we know there's no way we'd be here without you.

Writing this book was a journey we will never forget, and now that we have returned safely from the adventure, we can tell you that the best part is crafting the credits pages and sharing the credits with those who made this journey possible. So the next time you are watching a movie or reading a good book, take a moment to sit through the credits until the screen fades to black—catch all the acknowledgments of the people who worked hard to make the magic happen.

Notes

Introduction: An Invitation to Join Us on an Adventure

1. Corrie ten Boom, *Each New Day: 365 Reflections to Strengthen Your Faith* (Grand Rapids: Revel, 2013), 78.

Chapter 1: The Future Belongs to the Curious

1. "Walt's Quotes," D23: The Official Disney Fan Club, https://d23.com/section/walt-disney-archives/walts-quotes/.
2. "International Space Station Facts and Figures," NASA, updated October 28, 2019, https://www.nasa.gov/feature/facts-and-figures.
3. "Explore Moon to Mars," NASA, updated March 4, 2020, https://www.nasa.gov/topics/moon-to-mars/lunar-gateway.
4. Kira Bindrim, "Long before iPhones, This 19th-Century Gadget Made Everyone a Mobile Addict," Quartz, June 19, 2017, https://qz.com/1007704/long-before-iphones-this-19th-century-gadget-made-everyone-a-mobile-addict/.

Chapter 2: Into the Unknown

1. Ernest Shackleton, *South! The Story of Shackleton's Last Expedition 1914–1917* (London: William Heinemann, 1919), 168.
2. "Lieutenant Shackleton's Antarctic Expedition," *Science* 29, no. 746 (1909): 606–607. Accessed May 25, 2020, www.jstor.org/stable/1634583.
3. Andrew M. Carton and Brian J. Lucas, "How Can Leaders Overcome the Blurry Vision Bias? Identifying an Antidote to the Paradox of Vision Communication," *Academy of Management Journal* 61, no. 6 (2018): 2107, https://journals.aom.org/doi/10.5465/amj.2015.0375.
4. Wendy Lynn Schultz, "The History of Futures," in *The Future of Futures*, ed. Andrew Curry (Association of Professional Futurists, 2012), 3–7, https://www.researchgate.net/publication/272195683_The_History_of_Futures.
5. A good overview of these approaches can be found in *Thinking About the Future: Guidelines for Strategic Foresight*, ed. Andy Hines and Peter Bishop (Washington, DC: Social Technologies, 2006).
6. "Insight to a Dream: How It All Began. Walt Disney's Unique Vision Finds a Home in France with Disneyland Paris," Disneyland Paris Press News, September 10, 2015, https://web.archive.org/web/20160104120644/https://news.disneylandparis.com/en/2015/09/10/insight-to-a-dream-how-it-all-began-walt-disneys-unique-vision-finds-a-home-in-france-with-disneyland-paris/.

7. Peter C. Bishop and Andy Hines, *Teaching about the Future* (New York: Palgrave Macmillan, 2012), 3.
8. Eudie Pak, "Walt Disney's Rocky Road to Success," Biography.com, June 27, 2019, https://www.biography.com/news/walt-disney-failures.

Chapter 3: The Four Forces

1. Jonathan Swift, *The Works of Dr. Jonathan Swift, Dean of St. Patrick's Dublin*, vol. 8 (Edinburgh: A. Donaldson, 1761), 301.
2. Ray Kurzweil, "The Law of Accelerating Returns," KurzweilAI.net, March 7, 2001, http://www.kurzweilai.net/the-law-of-accelerating-returns.

Chapter 4: The Eight Intersections

1. Steve Jobs, "There's Sanity Returning," interview by Andy Reinhardt, *Business Week*, May 25, 1998.

Chapter 5: Identify

1. Tim Keller is paraphrasing Kierkegaard. Tim Keller, *The Reason for God: Belief in an Age of Skepticism* (New York: Penguin Books, 2008), 171.
2. Dan Gilbert, "The Psychology of Your Future Self," TED, March 2014, https://www.ted.com/talks/dan_gilbert_the_psychology_of_your_future_self.
3. Joel Beeke, "Jesus' Threefold Office as Prophet, Priest, and King," Ligonier Ministries, April 8, 2016, https://www.ligonier.org/blog/jesus-threefold-office-prophet-priest-and-king/.
4. Father Philip-Michael F. Tangorra, "Jesus Christ: Priest, Prophet, and King," *Homiletic & Pastoral Review*, October 25, 2013, https://www.hprweb.com/2013/10/jesus-christ-priest-prophet-and-king/.
5. Ibid.
6. This concept is rooted in Ezekiel 22:30, where God is looking for someone to step into the spaces in the wall on behalf of the people, in defense of their community. Those who stood on the wall could see the advancing attackers and could warn the citizens of what was coming.
7. Ibid.
8. Timothy Paul Jones, "Don't Use Prophet, Priest, and King as a Modern Leadership Typology," The Gospel Coalition, August 30, 2018, https://www.thegospelcoalition.org/article/prophet-priest-king-leadership-typology/.
9. Mark J. Perry, "Only 53 US Companies Have Been on the Fortune 500 since 1955, Thanks to the Creative Destruction That Fuels Economic Prosperity," AEI, May 23, 2018, https://www.aei.org/publication/only-53-us-companies-have-been-on-the-fortune-500-since-1955-thanks-to-the-creative-destruction-that-fuels-economic-prosperity/.
10. Richard Duppa and Quatremère de Quincy, *The Lives and Works of Michael Angelo and Raphael* (London: Bell & Daldy, 1872), 15.

Chapter 6: Relate

1. Charles Haddon Spurgeon, *Brilliants: Selected from the Works of C.H. Spurgeon* (Charleston, SC: Nabu Press, 2010), 20.

2. Michel Siffre, "Caveman: An Interview with Michel Siffre," interview by Joshua Foer, *Cabinet*, Summer 2018, http://www.cabinetmagazine.org/issues/30/foer.php.

3. Ibid.

4. Larry Getlen, "This Explorer Discovered Human Time Warp by Living in a Cave," *New York Post*, January 22, 2017, https://nypost.com/2017/01/22/this-explorer-discovered-human-time-warp-by-living-in-a-cave/.

5. Emma Barrett and Paul Martin, "A Scientist Spent 6 Months Alone in a Dark Cave to Study the Effects of Extreme Isolation," Business Insider, July 11, 2016, https://www.businessinsider.com/what-happens-in-extreme-isolation-2016-7.

6. Shasta Nelson, *Frientimacy: How to Deepen Friendships for Lifelong Health and Happiness* (Berkeley, CA: Seal Press, 2016), 32.

7. Lexico, s.v. "proximity," https://www.lexico.com/definition/proximity.

8. Laura Silver, "Smartphone Ownership Is Growing Rapidly around the World, but Not Always Equally," Pew Research Center, February 5, 2019, https://www.pewresearch.org/global/2019/02/05/smartphone-ownership-is-growing-rapidly-around-the-world-but-not-always-equally/.

9. Tae Yoo, "The Power of a Connected World," World Economic Forum, April 30, 2014, https://www.weforum.org/agenda/2014/04/technology-data-connected-world/.

10. Matthew D. Lieberman, *Social: Why Our Brains Are Wired to Connect* (New York: Crown Publishers, 2013).

11. Marina Rose, "The Science of Human Connection and Wellness in a Digitally Connected World," *Thrive Global* (blog), Medium, October 5, 2017, https://medium.com/thrive-global/the-science-of-human-connection-and-wellness-in-a-digitally-connected-world-611eb8c1b51c.

12. Shauna Niequist, *Bittersweet: Thoughts on Change, Grace, and Learning the Hard Way* (Grand Rapids: Zondervan, 2010), 188.

13. Emily Esfahani Smith, "Social Connection Makes a Better Brain," *The Atlantic*, October 29, 2013, https://www.theatlantic.com/health/archive/2013/10/social-connection-makes-a-better-brain/280934/.

14. IDEO, *Human-Centered Design Toolkit: An Open-Source Toolkit to Inspire New Solutions in the Developing World*, 2nd ed. (Canada: IDEO, 2011), 89.

Chapter 7: Belong

1. C. S. Lewis, *The Last Battle*, vol. 7, *The Chronicles of Narnia* (New York: Harper-Collins, 1956), 196.

2. "San Ysidro Land Port of Entry," U.S. General Services Administration, accessed May 3, 2020, https://www.gsa.gov/about-us/regions/welcome-to-the-pacific-rim-region-9/land-ports-of-entry/san-ysidro-land-port-of-entry.

3. "Did You Know . . . Century-Old Obelisks Mark U.S.-Mexican Border Line?," U.S. Customs and Border Protection, last modified December 20, 2019, https://www.cbp.gov/about/history/did-you-know/obelisk.

4. "Boundary," National Geographic, May 16, 2011, https://www.nationalgeo graphic.org/encyclopedia/boundary/.
5. Ron Garan, "The Orbital Perspective," *HuffPost* (blog), February 3, 2015, last updated April 5, 2015, https://www.huffpost.com/entry/the-orbital-perspective_b_6598558.
6. Ali Llewellyn, "The Collaboration Project," Open NASA, December 1, 2011, https://open.nasa.gov/blog/the-collaboration-project/.
7. How Chuang Chua, "The Importance of the Global Church," Crossway, June 10, 2018, https://www.crossway.org/articles/the-importance-of-the-global-church/.

Chapter 8: Gather

1. Stanley Hauerwas, *In Good Company: The Church as Polis* (Notre Dame, IN: University of Notre Dame Press, 1995), 157.
2. Melanie Kirkpatrick, "A Hymn's Long Journey Home," *The Wall Street Journal*, November 19, 2005, https://www.wsj.com/articles/SB113234570513601660.
3. Lexico, s.v. "congregation," https://www.lexico.com/en/definition/congregation.
4. "Karkhana Rover," YouTube video, 2:57, April 30, 2013, https://www.youtube.com/watch?v=7lQCLsw-5yA.

Chapter 9: Design

1. Peter Drucker, quoted in William A. Cohen, *Drucker on Leadership: New Lessons from the Father of Modern Management* (San Francisco: Jossey-Bass, 2010), 4.
2. Rikke Friis Dam and Teo Yu Siang, "Design Thinking: Getting Started with Empathy," Interaction Design Foundation, https://www.interaction-design.org/literature/article/design-thinking-getting-started-with-empathy.
3. Design Kit, "What Is Human-Centered Design?," IDEO.org, accessed April 21, 2020, https://www.designkit.org/human-centered-design.
4. Ibid.
5. "Agile Product Management with Scrum in a Nutshell," Visual Paradigm, accessed April 21, 2020, https://www.visual-paradigm.com/scrum/agile-project-management-in-nutshell/.
6. Friis Dam and Teo, "Design Thinking: Getting Started with Empathy."
7. Eric Ries, "The Lean Startup Methodology," The Lean Startup, accessed April 21, 2020, http://theleanstartup.com/principles.
8. In *The New Quotable Einstein* (Princeton, NJ: Princeton University Press, 2005), Alice Calaprice suggests that this quote is a paraphrase of two other quotes attributed to Einstein in 1946, which include: "The significant problems we face cannot be solved at the same level of thinking we were at when we created them" and "The world we have created today as a result of our thinking thus far has problems which cannot be solved by thinking the way we thought when we created them."
9. Ries, "The Lean Startup Methodology."

Chapter 10: Collaborate

1. Joseph P. Lash, *Helen and Teacher: The Story of Helen Keller and Anne Sullivan Macy* (New York: Delacorte Press, 1980), 489.

2. Louise Bruton, "The War at Sea," January 29, 2014, British Library, https://www.bl.uk/world-war-one/articles/the-war-at-sea.

3. Charlie Auvermann, interview by Ali Llewellyn, May 2014.

4. Phillips Payson O'Brien, *How the War Was Won: Air-Sea Power and Allied Victory in World War II* (Cambridge, UK: Cambridge University Press, 2015), 1.

5. Sarah Kellser, "IBM, Remote-Work Pioneer, Is Calling Thousands of Employees Back to the Office," *Quartz*, March 21, 2017, https://qz.com/924167/ibm-remote-work-pioneer-is-calling-thousands-of-employees-back-to-the-office/.

6. Jesse Lyn Stoner, "Let's Stop Confusing Cooperation and Teamwork with Collaboration," *Jesse Lyn Stoner on Leadership* (blog), Seapoint Center for Collaborative Leadership, accessed April 22, 2020, https://seapointcenter.com/cooperation-teamwork-and-collaboration/.

7. Ibid.

8. Ibid.

9. Tim O'Reilly, "Chapter 2. Government as a Platform," O'Reilly Media, https://www.oreilly.com/library/view/open-government/9781449381936/ch02.html.

10. "Thomas Jefferson to Joseph C. Cabell" in Andrew A. Lipscomb and Albert Ellery Bergh, eds., *The Writings of Thomas Jefferson* (Washington, DC: Thomas Jefferson Memorial Association, 1905), vol. 1, ch. 4, doc. 34, http://press-pubs.uchicago.edu/founders/documents/v1ch4s34.html.

11. "Open Government Declaration," Open Government Partnership, September 2011, https://www.opengovpartnership.org/process/joining-ogp/open-government-declaration/.

12. Nick Skytland, "We're in This Together: Why Mass Collaboration Is Changing Our Approach to Problem Solving in Government," Open NASA, November 5, 2012, https://open.nasa.gov/blog/were-in-this-together-why-mass-collaboration-is-changing-our-approach-to-problem-solving-in-government/.

Chapter 11: Scale

1. C. S. Lewis, *The Joyful Christian: 127 Readings* (New York: Simon & Schuster, 1977), 138.

2. Lauren Boucher, "What Is Exponential Growth?," *PopEd Blog*, Population Education, March 19, 2015, https://populationeducation.org/exponential-growth-and-doubling-time/.

3. Ray Kurzweil, "The Law of Accelerating Returns," KurzweilAI.net, March 7, 2001, https://www.kurzweilai.net/the-law-of-accelerating-returns.

4. "GDG Chapters Worldwide," Google Developers, Google, accessed April 23, 2020, https://developers.google.com/community/gdg/directory/.

5. Marshall McLuhan, *Understanding the Media: The Extensions of Man* (Cambridge, MA: MIT Press, 1994), 7.

6. Rick Warren, *The Purpose-Driven Life: What on Earth Am I Here For?* (Grand Rapids: Zondervan, 2012), 21.

7. Mark W. Breneman, "Technology + Ministry = Change," *InterVarsity Collegiate Ministries* (blog), October 21, 2016, https://collegiateministries.intervarsity.org/blog/technology-ministry-change.

8. Ibid.

9. Laura Silver, "Smartphone Ownership Is Growing Rapidly around the World, but Not Always Equally," Pew Research Center, February 5, 2019, https://www.pewresearch.org/global/2019/02/05/smartphone-ownership-is-growing-rapidly-around-the-world-but-not-always-equally/.

10. Breneman, "Technology + Ministry = Change."

11. Kelvin Salton do Prado, "Steganography: Hiding an Image Inside of Another," Towards Data Science, March 18, 2018, https://towardsdatascience.com/steganography-hiding-an-image-inside-another-77ca66b2acb1.

12. Jeremy Myers, "Exponential Church Growth," Redeeming God, https://redeeminggod.com/exponential-church-growth/.

13. "The UUPG List," Finishing the Task, last updated July 1, 2020, https://www.finishingthetask.com/about-finishing-the-task/people-group-list/.

Chapter 12: Impact

1. Anne Frank, *Anne Frank's Tales from the Secret Annex: A Collection of Her Short Stories, Fables, and Lesser-Known Writings,* ed. Gerrold van der Stroom, trans. Susan Massotty (London: Halban Publishers, 2010), 114.

2. John Wallert, Claes Held, Guy Madison, and Erik M. G. Olsson, "Temporal Changes in Myocardial Infarction Incident Rates Are Associated with Periods of Perceived Psychosocial Stress: A SWEDEHEART National Registry Study," *American Heart Journal* 191 (September 2017): 12–20, https://www.sciencedirect.com/science/article/pii/S0002870317301709.

3. Christa Sgobba, "Here's When You're Most and Least Likely to Have a Heart Attack," *Men's Health,* July 11, 2017, https://www.menshealth.com/health/a19524979/heart-attack-timing/.

4. Barry Schwartz, *Why We Work* (New York: TED Books, 2015), 3.

5. Michael Steger, "Creating Meaning and Purpose at Work," in *The Wiley Blackwell Handbook of the Psychology of Positivity and Strengths-Based Approaches at Work,* ed. Lindsay G. Oades, Michael Steger, Antonelle Delle Fave, and Jonathan Passmore (Malden, MA: John Wiley & Sons, 2017), https://www.researchgate.net/publication/310598648_Creating_Meaning_and_Purpose_at_Work.

6. Cone Communications, "2016 Cone Communications Millennial Employee Engagement Study," November 2, 2016, http://www.conecomm.com/research-blog/2016-millennial-employee-engagement-study.

7. "Ashes to Ashes," Literary Devices, accessed April 24, 2020, https://literarydevices.net/ashes-to-ashes/.

8. Kirsten Weir, "More than Job Satisfaction," *Monitor on Psychology* 44, no. 11 (December 2013), 39, https://www.apa.org/monitor/2013/12/job-satisfaction.

9. Nick Craig and Scott A. Snook, "From Purpose to Impact," *Harvard Business Review* (May 2014), https://hbr.org/2014/05/from-purpose-to-impact.

10. Ibid.

11. Vocabulary.com, s.v. "vocation," https://www.vocabulary.com/dictionary/vocation.
12. Bill Denzel and David Kinnaman, "Why We're Studying Vocation and Work," Barna Group, September 18, 2018, https://www.barna.com/vocation-and-work/.
13. "Creating a Culture of Calling," Lord of Life Lutheran Church, accessed April 24, 2020, https://lordoflifeva.org/C3.
14. Frederick Buechner, *Wishful Thinking: A Seeker's ABC* (New York: HarperCollins, 1993), 95.
15. Ibid.
16. "Our Mission Statement," World Vision, accessed April 24, 2020, https://www.wvi.org/our-mission-statement.
17. Starbucks, "Living Our Values," Corporate Social Responsibility, Fiscal 2003 Annual Report, https://globalassets.starbucks.com/assets/e31d4604b78141bfb13172aa5fd67cfa.pdf.
18. "Our Mission," Starbucks Coffee Company, accessed April 25, 2020, https://www.starbucks.com/about-us/company-information/mission-statement.

Chapter 13: Curiosity in Action

1. Will Mancini, *God Dreams: 12 Vision Templates for Finding and Focusing Your Church's Future* (Nashville, TN: B&H Publishing Group, 2016), 40.
2. Bill Gates, quoted in Andrew M. Carton and Brian J. Lucas, "How Can Leaders Overcome the Blurry Vision Bias? Identifying an Antidote to the Paradox of Vision Communication," *Academy of Management Journal* 61, no. 6 (2018): 2106, https://journals.aom.org/doi/10.5465/amj.2015.0375.
3. Carton and Lucas, "How Can Leaders Overcome the Blurry Vision Bias?," 2106.
4. "Ford's Model T: A Car for the Great Multitude," *Past Forward* (blog), January 28, 2015, https://www.thehenryford.org/explore/blog/fords-model-t.
5. Mark 10:46–52 (NIV).
6. Jay Yarow, "Take a Sneak Peek at Microsoft's Vision of the House of the Future," Business Insider, July 18, 2013, https://www.businessinsider.com/inside-microsofts-house-of-the-future-2013-7.

Chapter 14: Paper Rockets

1. Antoine de Saint-Exupéry, *The Wisdom of the Sands*, trans. Stuart Gilbert (New York: Harcourt, Brace & Company, 1950), 155.
2. Colin Schultz, "Shackleton Probably Never Took Out an Ad Seeking Men for a Hazardous Journey," *Smithsonian* magazine, September 10, 2013, https://www.smithsonianmag.com/smart-news/shackleton-probably-never-took-out-an-ad-seeking-men-for-a-hazardous-journey-5552379/.
3. Joshua Horn, "Shackleton's Ad—Men Wanted for Hazardous Journey," Discerning History, May 15, 2013, http://discerninghistory.com/2013/05/shackletons-ad-men-wanted-for-hazardous-journey/.
4. George Savvas, "Getting Ready for Disneyland Park to Debut—a Look Back at July 17, 1955," *Disney Parks Blog*, July 17, 2011, https://disneyparks.disney

.go.com/blog/2011/07/getting-ready-for-disneyland-park-to-debut-a-look-back-at-july-17-1955/.

Chapter 15: Infinite Possiblities

1. Matthew 14:29.
2. Carey Nieuwhof, "Why Trust Matters More than You Realize (and 3 Ways to Create It When It's Not There)," CareyNieuwhof.com, June 7, 2014, https://careynieuwhof.com/trust-2/.

Acknowledgments

1. See H. W. Turnbull, ed., *The Correspondence of Isaac Newton: 1661–1675*, vol. 1 (London: Published for the Royal Society at the University Press, 1959), 416.

FOUR **FORCES**

How is the **PURPOSE** force driving change for you?

How is the **PEOPLE** force driving change for you?

How is the **PLACE** force driving change for you?

How is the **TECHNOLOGY** force driving change for you?

Futures Framework **WORKSHEET**

FUTURES **CANVAS**

What is your current MISSION statement?

To what community will you BELONG ?

How will you SCALE it ?

Where will you GATHER ?

What IMPACT will you have ?

How will you IDENTIFY ?

What will you DESIGN ?

Describe your PREFERRED FUTURE ?

Who will you RELATE with ?

How will you COLLABORATE ?

